TIME
KEEPERS

THE GREAT
TIME
KEEP

JAZZ DRUMMERS

LESLIE GOURSE

FRANKLIN **WATTS**

A Division of Grolier Publishing

New York · London · Hong Kong · Sydney
Danbury, Connecticut

The author would like to thank drummers Kenny Washington and
Malcolm Briggs for their information and advice on aspects of this book.

Visit Franklin Watts on the Internet at http//:publishing.grolier.com

Book design by John D. Sparks

Photographs ©: Bob Parent Photo Archive: 33, 35; Chuck Stewart: 45, 126; Corbis-
Bettmann: 8, 51, 57, 119 (UPI), 26, 48; Frank Driggs Collection: 12, 15, 19, 43, 53, 79, 109;
Lee Tanner: 115, 122; Raymond Ross Photography: 61 (Drum Sunday), 84 (Record), 22, 85;
Retna Ltd./Camera Press Ltd.: 95 (Andy Freeberg), 83 (William P. Gottlieb), 70
(Stills/Letto), 106 (Darryl Pitt), 66, 86, 92, 101 (David Redferns).

Library of Congress Cataloging-in-Publication Data
Gourse, Leslie
Timekeepers : the great jazz drummers / by Leslie Gourse.
p. cm. — (The art of jazz)
Includes bibliographical references and index.
Summary: Discusses the role of drumming in jazz and surveys some of the
greatest jazz drummers in history, from Warren Baby Dodds and
Arthur Zutty Singleton to Tony Williams and Elvin Jones.
ISBN 0-531-11564-X (lib. bdg.)   0-531-16405-5 (pbk.)
1. Drummers (Musicians) — Biography — Juvenile literature. 2. Jazz musicians —
Biography — Juvenile literature. 3. Jazz — History and criticism — Juvenile literature.
[1. Drummers. 2. Jazz — History and criticism.] I. Title. II. Series: Gourse, Leslie. Art of Jazz.
ML3929.G67   1999
786.9'165'0922 — dc21
[B]   98-40009
                                                                    CIP
                                                                  AC MN

CONTENTS

CHAPTER **ONE**
The Great Jazz Drummers

7

CHAPTER **TWO**
Warren "Baby" Dodds and
Arthur "Zutty" Singleton from New Orleans

18

CHAPTER **THREE**
Baby Dodds's Memories

25

CHAPTER **FOUR**
More about the Early Jazz Drummers

32

PART **ONE**
The Lesser-Known Early Jazz
and Swing-Era Drummers

32

PART **TWO**
The Masterful Swing-Era Drummers

40

CHAPTER **FIVE**
The Bebop Revolution

63

THE JAZZ DRUMMING TREE:
a concise history of the development
of jazz drumming   **78**

CHAPTER SIX
Latin Rhythms in the Bebop Era and Beyond   **88**

CHAPTER SEVEN
Hard Bop, Cool Jazz, and Third Stream Music   **93**

CHAPTER EIGHT
Tony Williams, Elvin Jones, and
Other Masters of Modern Drumming   **112**

SOURCE NOTES   **128**

SUGGESTED LISTENING   **133**

FOR MORE INFORMATION   **139**

INDEX   **142**

CHAPTER ONE

THE GREAT JAZZ DRUMMERS

Legendary actor Jimmy Stewart was cast in the role of an equally legendary swing-era bandleader in *The Glenn Miller Story*. Stewart played trombone on the same stage with trumpeter Louis Armstrong and drummer Gene Krupa. Afterward, Stewart's wife complimented him on his performance. He replied, "I don't kid myself. When I start playing jazz with fellas like Louis Armstrong and Gene Krupa, I'm lucky if I come in third." The comment testifies to the popularity and artistry of Gene Krupa, one of the best-known jazz musicians who ever lived. Jazz has had many fine players but relatively few superstars. Krupa numbered among them.

He was a handsome, flamboyant, dramatic performer. His long hair flew around, as he chewed gum, flailed his arms, kept the time, and drove groups to great heights of excitement. He supplied so much of the fireworks for clarinetist Benny Goodman's landmark concert in

Benny Goodman (on clarinet) and Gene Krupa

Carnegie Hall in January 1938 that, afterward, he and Goodman quarreled about who was more important. Goodman hated to be upstaged. Somewhat of an egotist himself, Krupa left Goodman's band.

Like all the best jazz drummers in each generation of players, Krupa had his own style, and he changed or broadened the scope of existing ideas about how to play time and rhythm. As a result, he enriched jazz. The best drummers have often also been melodic drummers. That means they have always kept in mind the melody of a song and enhanced it, interpreting the music instead of playing their own ideas for the sake of showing off.

Drummers don't actually play notes; they play tones. But the best drummers have either learned to read music, or they understand exactly what the other instrumentalists are playing and work with their groups closely. Drummers do tune their various drums to different pitches—though quite a few famous drummers, such as the beboppers Max Roach and Art Blakey, have said they don't care so much about the pitch of their drums as they do about the quality of their sound. Most drummers augment their drum sets with percussion instruments, and they decide for themselves how many drums of each type to use in their sets. There are no hard and fast rules about the equipment drummers must use, but customs have developed over time.

In the pre-history of jazz, singers and drummers in Africa performed together. Drummers played all sorts of percussion instruments and "talked" on their drums, tapping out speechlike messages about every aspect of their communal lives. When Africans were brought as slaves to North and South America, Central America, and the Caribbean, they brought their musical traditions with them. In each area of the "new world," slaves blended their musical, cultural, and spiritual ideas with the existing cultures—Portuguese in Brazil, Spanish (and Dutch and French, too) in much of Latin America, and British, French, and Spanish in the United States.

So powerful were the messages that Africans played on their drums that, before the Civil War in the United States, some slave states banned the manufacture and use of African drums. One jazz writer, Len Lyons, called the law a violation of free speech.[1]

But no law could ever destroy the power and fascination of the drums. More than any other instrument, drums can mimic and quicken the human heartbeat. At the sound of the drums, people can forget about everything but how thrilling it is to be alive, to strive for self-expression and freedom. In New Orleans, by the mid-nineteenth century, one of the most popular events attended by both whites and Africans was an African *vodun* (voodoo) ceremony, with hypnotic drumming conducted under the leadership of a priestess named Marie Laveau. People were carried away, sometimes into frenzies, by the rituals.

In Africa, several drummers played at the same time, using a variety of time signatures: usually 3/4 time, like a waltz, which has three beats to a measure; and 6/8 time, a one-step, which means six eighth notes to a measure; and 4/4, a fox trot, which has four beats to a measure. (Measures, or bars, are used when music is written in the European tradition. Africans didn't write out their music; older people taught the new generations.)

In the United States, the many rhythms (polyrhythmic music) of Africa were simplified as jazz developed in the first twenty years of the twentieth century in New Orleans. There the bands played a basic march rhythm, in 4/4 time, with the added, lilting touch of swing. It not only stressed the weak beat in the measure for syncopation but added a variety of accents all around the march beat. Public funerals with marching bands became very popular in New Orleans. People joined clubs, secret societies, or lodges and planned their wakes and funeral processions in detail. On the way to the cemetery, marching bands played slow dirges in 4/4 time—hymns such as "Nearer My God to Thee." But on the way back from the cemetery, the bands broke loose with an entirely different sound.

As Bunk Johnson, a leading early jazz trumpeter in New Orleans, explained about the return trip, "We'd go right on into ragtime—what the people call today swing-ragtime. We would play 'Didn't He Ramble,' or we'd take all those spiritual hymns and turn them into ragtime—2/4 movements, you know, step lively everybody. 'Didn't He Ramble,' 'When the Saints Go Marching In,' that good old piece, 'Ain't Gonna Study War No More,' and several others we would have and we'd play them just for that effect.

"We would have a Second Line there that was most equivalent to King Rex parade—Mardi Gras Carnival parade. The police were unable to keep the Second Line back—all in the street, all on the sidewalks, in front of the band, and behind the lodge, in front of the lodge. We'd have some immense crowds following. They would follow the funeral up to the cemetery just to get this ragtime music comin' back. . . . Even police horse[s] . . . would prance. Music done them all the good in the world. That's the class of music we used on funerals."[2]

The Second Line of dancers and musicians was unique to New Orleans. And though the drummers still played in 4/4 time for the procession, they accented the rhythm in such a way that it sounded as if the drummers were playing in 2/4 time; they called it the feeling of "playing in two," and it was unique to New Orleans. As the years passed, the intensity and complexity of the rhythms for the fresh, expressive music— jazz—kept increasing. Musicians kept building upon the original sparkle of syncopation, playing longer lines and smoothing out the rhythms by the 1930s, and more development continued for many years to come.

It's a great leap from the early jazz drummers to the modernists at the end of the century. The first jazz drummers kept time clearly on the bass drum, concentrated on accompaniment, and invented the foundation and rudiments— the techniques and the technical facility—for the art of jazz drumming.

Drumming based on jazz traditions has become so complex that modernists actually concentrate on soloing, coloring, and accenting a group's music. They perform in such complex ways that they become percussionists, not strictly drummers. Modern drummers rooted in jazz traditions play the bass drum subtly and unobtrusively, using the foot pedal, to "feather"—stroke—the bass drum lightly in 4/4 time. At the same time, their hands move all over the drum set and cymbals, playing intricate, creative, often very exciting improvisations. In modern mainstream jazz groups, the bassist, not the drummer, has become the primary timekeeper. And drummers in an experimental style called free jazz, which emerged in the late 1950s, function completely as colorists, accenters, and soloists, moving around their equipment in very abstract ways, improvising spontaneously, without playing the foundation of 4/4 time on the bass drum or ever functioning as timekeepers at all. Free jazz drummers, even more frequently than drummers in modern mainstream groups, are often referred to as percussionists, since their total responsibility is to play fills, accents and colors, not time.

Mainstream music is obviously rooted in jazz traditions. At times, but not always, drummers work in full cooperation with bassists. For example, the feathered bass drum work gives bassists a center to return to after they venture afield to solo. But modern drummers—mainstream and experimental—have far more freedom than the early drummers.

The first *radical* change from the New Orleans style was heralded by a drummer named Papa Jo Jones in the 1930s in Count Basie's band. Jones kept time on the hi-hat cymbals—two cymbals facing each other

Papa Jo Jones with Count Basie's band

in the style of a clam shell, mounted on a metal stand, and operated by a foot pedal. The hi-hat gave Jo Jones greater fluidity and flexibility for the tempos he played. It could make a variety of sounds, from sighs and whispers to snaps and clicks.

By the 1940s, following in Jones's footsteps, all drummers kept time on the cymbals, particularly on the top, ride cymbal of the drum set, and used the bass drum for accents. Those accents were called "bombs," and the beboppers called their technique "dropping bombs." One should remember that these drummers didn't abandon the bass drum. They still played four beats to the bar on the bass, but they did it subtly, "feathering" the bass lightly with the foot pedal.

After the beboppers came the diverse styles of the 1950s, such as hard bop, cool jazz, and Third Stream Music. The drummers played their own embellishments—with gospel and blues feeling for hard bop, mellow lines for the cool school, and European classical influences for Third Stream Music—all firmly rooted in bebop innovations for time-keeping, accenting, and coloring.

Then came the very influential drummer Elvin Jones, a truly modern percussionist. He was still playing mainstream jazz but with enormous individuality and greater freedom than ever in his ideas for accompaniment and solos. He achieved fame for his powerful playing in saxophonist John Coltrane's group in the 1960s, mesmerizing audiences with his looseness and creativity. He would continue his innovative freedom as leader of his own groups. And he would influence all the young jazz drummers yet to come.

With the advent of free jazz groups in the late 1950s and 1960s, the drummers became co-equals with all the other members of the group, playing along with everyone else in an ensemble, not simply accompanying. There is no set time for free jazz drummers to keep, and they are noted for their surrealistic flow of sound. No longer do they hold a band together, as they did when they were cast in their classic role of time-keepers in jazz groups.

And so, like the composition of drum sets, the techniques and emphases of drummers have evolved enormously. Overall, there have been as many ways to approach drum sets and percussion instruments as there have been drummers. Performers are always influenced by the changing tastes of audiences, the demands of the music the musicians play, and their own ideas.

For example, an early drummer might typically have used a big bass drum, a snare drum, one or two tom-toms on the right-hand side of the set, and two cymbals on top, without any hi-hat cymbals. Many of the earliest drummers didn't even use brushes, only drumsticks. (Brushes are wire or plastic whisks bound together.) Warren "Baby" Dodds, one of the first, finest, and best-known drummers to come from New Orleans, disliked brushes so much that he learned to play very lightly with only the sticks.[3] For one thing, early recording techniques were so primitive that brushes tended to sound like odd noisemakers rather than rhythm tools. So the first drummers preferred the highly defined, dancing sound of sticks.

Later, more modern drummers prided themselves on their artistry and subtlety with brushes. The current generation of jazz drummers plays with brushes sparingly—though they are still used for songs that require that soft sound. (One reason drummers use brushes less frequently is that the contemporary public has developed a taste for loud music.)

Early jazz drummers always used calfskin heads for their drums; modern drummers use plastic heads. Early drummers such as Baby Dodds played entire solos on the wooden rims of their bass and snare drums. Modern drummers wouldn't dream of doing that. The rims of their drums are made of plastic, not wood, and the sound is quite different.

In the course of developing drums and other percussion instruments, inventors improved the construction of the bass and snare drums and tom-toms. And the Chinese, Turkish, and other cultures (including Europe and the Americas) make highly prized cymbals of varying sizes and delicacy that augment drum sets and provide drummers with a wide variety of sounds and choices. In the 1940s, some of the drums began to get smaller or thinner, and some cymbals became bigger.

In the swing era, young drummers marveled at the elaborate array of drums and percussion instruments collected by the masterful drummer and showman Sonny Greer for Duke Ellington's band. It boggles the

Sonny Greer (right) with Duke Ellington

mind to consider how Greer ever managed to play all his equipment—a bass drum, a snare drum, a tom-tom, a floor tom-tom, a Chinese cymbal, a Turkish cymbal, a small splash cymbal set high on the equipment and used for accents, and hi-hat cymbals, cowbells, huge round tam-tams set high at the back of his set, tubular bells, a woodblock, a set of five temple blocks, drum sticks, brushes, and timpani mallets, a pair of tub-shaped timpani, and a vibraphone.[4] Some sources say he also used chimes and a gong. Sonny's set had his own initials on the drums. (Previously, drums were usually decorated with a scene and lit from within by an electric bulb. That heat helped keep away the dampness, but created the problem of dryness affecting calfskin.)

Some jazz drummers have always preferred a pared-down, essential set, and they have proved that a drummer doesn't need an enormous array to play interesting music. With only a few pieces, Ben Riley in the 1960s brilliantly interpreted pianist and composer Thelonious Monk's very complex music. Other drummers always embellish their basic sets of bass, snare, tom-toms, and cymbals with bells and woodblocks and exotic percussion instruments drawn from many cultures. Marvin "Smitty" Smith, a youngster who became one of the most prominent jazz drummers based in New York beginning in 1982, has augmented his drum set with a fascinating array of percussion instruments. And it's not unusual to see a rock drummer, or a rock-jazz drummer in a fusion group, using electric as well as acoustic instruments, with a fifteen-piece drum set. However, these drummers don't always use every piece in performances. Sometimes a huge drum set is used only for the sake of the grandeur of its visual impression.

All drummers, from the New Orleans players to the modernists, have had to take special pains to build their own sets, often adding pieces from all over the world and coddling their expensive equipment lovingly. The early drummers virtually made their own drums, obtaining the pieces and putting them together. Modernists must work hard simply to maintain their drum sets in top-flight shape. A little neglect can lead to the destruction of a drum head or the delicate alloys used to manufacture cymbals.

Latin and South American drummers and percussionists have their own panoply of instruments. Best known to North American audiences are the conga drums, bongos, and timbales. Chapter six in this book will explain the world of Latin rhythms—particularly the Cuban creations.

This book will not teach anyone technical lessons about how to play jazz drums but will trace the history of the major innovators and stylists, who developed increasingly fiery and faster tempos and more complex patterns, accents, and embellishments. For more information about the evolution of jazz styles and some basic techniques, or rudiments, of jazz drumming, read this book's Jazz Drumming Tree now.

CHAPTER

WARREN "BABY" DODDS AND ARTHUR "ZUTTY" SINGLETON FROM NEW ORLEANS

TWO

WARREN "BABY" DODDS

Two modern jazz musicians, horn player Loren Schoenberg and drummer/bandleader Mel Lewis, did a radio series on jazz drums over a period of months in the late 1980s on WKCR, Columbia University's station in New York.[1] They began with Warren "Baby" Dodds, born in New Orleans on Christmas Eve 1894. He was nicknamed Baby because his father's name was also Warren, but Baby was destined to be regarded as the father of jazz drumming.

Schoenberg and Lewis played a recording of Baby playing on a complete drum set, taking a solo on the wooden rims of the bass and snare drums. New Orleans drummers especially liked drum sets emphasizing those pieces. With them, Baby performed a tap dance in perfect time throughout a whole song. He, like other New Orleans drummers, also used a variety of cowbells. His drums definitely had

Baby Dodds (on drums) with King Creole's Jazz Band

calfskins on them. His cowbells were tuned beautifully. And he knew exactly what sounds he would get out of his rims. He used cymbals sparingly and had little interest in the sock cymbal or, as it would come to be called, the hi-hat. Not until the 1930s did drummers make it a staple of their equipment. But Baby was primarily a rhythmic player, who kept the beat on the bass drum.

Modern drummers would eventually use plastic drum heads instead of calfskins, because, although the early drummers could get a beautiful sound with calfskin drumheads, there were drawbacks, too. For one thing, weather affects calfskin. If the tone of a bass drum with calfskins sounded as if the drum was very tight, it was most likely because the drummer was playing in a place with dry heat—indoors in winter, outdoors in summer. Baby had to contend with the problems posed by the weather. Even so, every strike on his bass drum was absolutely even and controlled, as he played four beats to the bar and remained at the same dynamic level; he could play four beats to the bar for three or four minutes straight, and he played other parts of his drum set over that bass drum beat.

The recording of Dodds on the WKCR show was done in 1940 in a group led by soprano saxophone master Sidney Bechet in Chicago. By that time, Baby had already been established for about twenty years as the most influential New Orleans drummer. The song selected as one example of Baby's best playing was called "Stompy Jones." Record companies wouldn't let Baby or any drummer emphasize, or in some cases even use, drums at all for recordings. The drums were too overwhelming, recording engineers said. And so on this tune, Baby played a wood block and drum rims for his solo. Then he settled back into the snare drum and the press roll (a rudiment of drumming) and one eight-bar phrase where he played the ride cymbal.

Baby played at a perfect level, compensating for what the recording engineer didn't know about the sound of the drums. In those days, engineers did all recording in monophonic, not stereophonic sound, and a musician used one microphone to accomplish all the balancing.

Mel Lewis tried to explain the art and priorities of the first jazz drummers compared with the work of modern drummers. The old drummers valued teamwork. Mel said, "Today everybody plays a solo from the down beat [the first beat of a measure, or, as implied here, the start of the song], and drummers stick every idea they can think of into their work from the down beat. [But] the whole [point] is to be an accompanist. [Baby] was an accompanist and swung the soloist, playing under him, and swung his solos. Today everybody overplays. There's too much based on technique: how fast can I do this? how many notes can I get in on one bar?" Lewis complained that young, modern drummers didn't seem able to play four beats on the bass drum evenly.

Baby felt drummers should accompany and support groups led by such front-line instrumentalists as clarinetists, trumpeters, trombonists, and violinists. And although he himself led his own trio recorded by the Circle label, sometimes now available on other labels, he didn't even think drummers should lead their own groups. He made these pronouncements in his biography, *The Baby Dodds Story*.[2]

ARTHUR "ZUTTY" SINGLETON

An early friend of Louis Armstrong, Zutty Singleton, born in Bunkie, Louisiana, in 1898, grew up in New Orleans, where he played with Armstrong and listened to Baby Dodds for inspiration. Zutty may have heard Baby for the first time when Baby played drums in Fate Marable's band on the Mississippi riverboats, between 1918 and 1921, along with Louis "Satchmo" Armstrong. Later in the 1920s, Zutty played in Fate Marable's band himself and migrated to Chicago, the center of the jazz world by then. Zutty played there with Louis Armstrong in clubs and in Armstrong's Hot Five and Hot Seven studio groups. They made classic recordings on the Okeh label in Chicago in 1928.

Among Zutty's other early recordings was "Savoyager's Stomp," with a popular big band led by Carroll Dickerson. Satchmo and pianist Earl Hines played for the date, too. Zutty also played with a small group for a recording of "St. James Infirmary" in The Savoy Ballroom Five with Armstrong and Hines. He was restricted from using the bass drum, or at most he used brushes on it—the metal brushes popular in the era.

Zutty also recorded the classic song well-loved by other musicians, "After You've Gone," with the bright, starring trumpeter/leader Roy Eldridge in 1936. Zutty played snare drums, at a good tempo for those days—not very fast, in 4/4 time, with a wonderful sound and with press rolls and a back beat at the same time, hitting the rim while he played the roll. The roll, a series of uninterrupted beats free of rhythmic stresses, gave the song the propulsion, while the back beat, played on the snare drum on the second and fourth beats, gave it a high—a lift.[3]

Zutty Singleton

Zutty also recorded with trumpeter Henry "Red" Allen, trombonist Benny Morton, and clarinetist Edmond Hall on "King Porter Stomp," for which he may have used a hi-hat cymbal. It was invented in essentially its modern, current form in 1927.[4] But he concentrated on the snare drums. And on another recording, called "About Face," done with trumpeter Joe Sullivan and clarinetist Pee Wee Russell, Zutty played tom-toms, with a leathery sound from the calfskin.

Baby and Zutty, the New Orleans-nurtured jazz drum pioneers, lived very hard lives. Baby acquired his drum set by painstaking work over a period of years; he saved pennies to be able to afford to buy the pieces one by one. He recalled in his biography the rough times he spent in the Storyville district of New Orleans, where one girlfriend actually wanted to kill him.

Musicians were held in low esteem. Baby himself freely admitted that he drank too much from a very young age and noticed that musicians everywhere were often high-strung and bad-tempered. But through all the rough lessons he learned, he concentrated on developing his art and technique. And he believed that groups couldn't play well together unless musicians felt spiritual harmony with one another. Most often, they rose above the hardships of their lives to try to play their best.

Baby might have received a bit more of the credit for pioneering as a jazz drummer than the younger Zutty Singleton did. Both of them traveled in essentially the same circles, particularly in Chicago, where they often played with many of the same musicians. Baby Dodds played in Louis Armstrong's Hot Seven studio groups in 1927 and Zutty played for the Hot Seven in 1928. Neither drummer got enough credit or financial rewards for his work while he was in his prime. Baby Dodds, sick from strokes and mostly inactive throughout the 1950s, died in 1959. Zutty Singleton received a Gene Krupa Award in 1974 and then was voted into the National Association of Recording Arts and Sciences Hall of Fame in 1975 for his work on Louis Armstrong's Hot Five recordings. But Zutty had already suffered a stroke in 1969, before the awards came. He and his wife Marge lived on very little money in New York, where they had settled. He died there in 1975.

Drummer Mel Lewis, who was born in Buffalo, New York, in 1929, and therefore was more than thirty years younger than Zutty and Baby, recalled the few times he saw or heard the old masters. By the time he became very familiar with their work, they were well past their heydays. "I saw Zutty at the Metropole [a popular, if unfashionable club on Broadway near Times Square]," said Mel. "Gene [Krupa] would be working there, and on the same bill. A lot of times, I would hang with Gene, and sometimes we would go down and hear Zutty."

A great deal of the art of jazz drums was passed down in this way, in the African tradition, with the elders teaching the youngsters. Mel emphasized the work of Baby and Zutty in the 1920s and 1930s: "This was basic drumming being created at the moment. They were able to create something new each time they played. And they had to learn on their own." Their primary guides, when they were learning to play in New Orleans around 1915, were the military marching bands and show drummers. Baby himself recalled playing a snare drum in the Second Line in traditional funerals.

At the end of the twentieth century, excellent jazz drummers are still using some traces of the techniques that Baby Dodds originated and favored for his accompaniment and for the fills and breaks that served as the foundation for the highly developed art of the drum solo. Modern drummers would use all parts of their drum sets and broaden the reach of the earliest jazz drummers beyond what they could possibly have imagined.

CHAPTER THREE

BABY DODDS'S MEMORIES

In his biography, Baby Dodds's gave a clear picture of what it was like to grow up poor, musically gifted, and ambitious in a city of music lovers. His older brother, Johnny, played the clarinet, and Baby wanted to study the flute. But he knew African-Americans had no chances of finding work in the classical music world. "I always liked symphonies and still do," he said. "When I hear a symphony I pick out different things which I feel I can use in jazz. . . . I used to carry any melody on the snare drum that a band played. I got that idea from listening to symphonic music and also from playing in street parades. . . ."[1]

His father wouldn't buy him a drum, so Baby went to work for "four dollars and six bits a week," he said, until he saved enough money to buy a snare drum and drumsticks. Then he found a slightly better job in a factory and saved money for an old-fashioned bass drum. Eventu-

Baby Dodds

ally he bought a foot pedal, "put the set together, and by gimmy, I come to make a noise!" he recalled.[2] In time, he added a cymbal, a wood block, a ratchet, and whistles, all bought in a pawnshop. He loved his set passionately.

Learning to play primarily by ear, he listened to the drummers in town who played in show bands and parades and sought out good teachers. One taught him to play on a drum pad; the second taught him to read music and play different patterns with his right hand (mammy) and his left hand (daddy) at the same time. From listening to drummer

Henry Martin, who played in the town's best band led by trombonist Kid Ory, Baby developed his smooth, flowing press roll. And like all drummers of his era, he learned how to tune his drums and put the heads on and tuck them in himself.

"And when I was learning, I picked up the different drum terms. . . . I learned that a biff shot was one abrupt fast lick, a flam is a sixteenth note, a flim flam is a thirty-second, and a lick is when you just hit the rim. With a lick you just hit it and with a biff you try to make it sound on something, either the rim or anything else solid. The pickup [downbeat] was the first beat and the rudiments are the things we did with a number to be played. It was just different things we did to make the number go and to make the other fellows play. In other words in a calm, ordinary way you push the number and the other musicians, too."[3]

He worked in all the traditional places for a jazz musician—lawn parties, fish fries, honky tonks in Storyville, which was the entertainment and red-light section of town—and he played in halls where he had to know the dance music of the day—mazurkas, quadrilles, polkas, and schottisches. In the parades, he played the snare drum, while someone else played the bass drum. That was how the responsibilities were divided in those days. And of course he played the blues in most places. All the while, he struggled to improve his technique.

Mingling with the legendary New Orleans musicians of the era, he especially revered his brother, John, who played clarinet with Kid Ory's band. Baby would always remember how musicians welcomed any new arrival hired for a group and how old-timers often encouraged him. But the musicians in Kid Ory's band, including Baby's brother, John, criticized Baby fiercely. When Baby sat in with that band, one by one the other musicians left the stand. Their coldness made Baby commit himself more than ever to playing better.

In 1917, after the secretary of the U.S. Navy closed down Storyville on moral grounds, Baby got a job through a friend, well-known New Orleans bassist Pops Foster, on a Mississippi riverboat. Many New Orleans musicians left town that way and eventually migrated to the

Southwest, Los Angeles, and Chicago, where they also found work. Baby recalled playing in Fate Marable's band on a boat with a dozen musicians including Louis Armstrong from 1918 to 1921: "The music would sound so pretty, especially on the water. . . . We had so much harmony in that band[4]. . . Streckfus [the owner of the riverboat line, bought Baby] a slide whistle and different little trinkets that were to go with my drums," Baby recalled. "That's what they call traps. A snare drum isn't a trap drum. Rather, traps are such things as blocks, triangles, slide whistles, horns, tambourines, cocoa blocks and things like that. In those days nobody handled these traps but the drummers. And if you couldn't handle the traps you didn't get a job."[5]

Baby learned a lot about music on the boat. Drum manufacturer William Ludwig came aboard and tailored a sock cymbal (hi-hat) to Baby's needs. "Two cymbals were set up and a foot pedal with them," Baby described. But Baby never got used to them. "Some drummers can't drum without them. I can't drum with them."[6]

And he recalled the hardships. He played for segregated audiences for most performances. On rare and happy occasions, African-Americans made up the whole audience, and the band could dance and feel free to mingle. But the band had to sleep in the ship's hold, and the men had only plain food to eat during months-long journeys. When he got a chance, Baby went ashore and ordered rice and beans and other food that reminded him of home.

Streckfus loved Baby's drumming. But eventually Baby and Louis Armstrong left the riverboat line because of a misunderstanding, Baby said, with the bosses about how musicians should play. "Some of the older people on the boat couldn't dance to our music and Streckfus wanted to introduce what he called toddle time. It was really two-four time but he wanted four beats to the measure. It's what they are doing today," Baby said, referring to the 1950s, when he dictated his biography. "To me, four beats was all wrong. It has a tendency to speed up the music. But for the older people it was easier since instead of dancing to a step, they would just bounce around. . . . And I just couldn't do this toddle time on my drums. I felt that it would change me so much. . . ." He and Louis Armstrong handed in their resignations on the first of September 1921.[7]

Baby was very sad about leaving the boat, but he soon joined the Joe "King" Oliver band in Los Angeles. Oliver, formerly the trumpeter in Kid Ory's band in New Orleans, had been Armstrong's mentor. Baby's brother John actually advised Oliver not to hire Baby in Los Angeles, because Baby liked to drink a lot of whiskey. Baby knew that was his weakness. But he had become a very good player, and King Oliver hired him. The band moved to Chicago. Hearing Baby play there, John was surprised and delighted—"dumbfounded,"[8] Baby recalled about the effect of his mature drumming style on John. Louis Armstrong joined the band, which played at the Lincoln Gardens on Chicago's South Side. Johnny Dodds joined the band, too. And the best musicians, white and African-American, went to hear it.

"Benny Goodman, Jess Stacy, Frank Teschemacher, Dave Tough, Bud Freeman, and Ben Pollack used to come to listen," Baby said, naming prominent white musicians. Both Davey Tough and Ben Pollack were drummers. Baby said of another white drummer, "George Wettling came when he was still in knee pants. . . . The band had everything so perfect that it was recognized as tops. We were getting fifty-five dollars a week at the time, and there were a lot of bands around that weren't getting half that. . . . One of the most frequent visitors at the Gardens was Paul Whiteman." Baby recounted how Whiteman, a very popular bandleader, and his band members, playing at a club that closed for the night before the Lincoln Gardens did, used to try to learn the music that Oliver was playing. But Oliver never told them the correct names of the songs. "That's how some of the numbers got different names," Baby recalled.[9]

Oliver wanted Baby to play with wire brushes, not just sticks, because Oliver wanted to lighten Baby's sound. But Baby played heavily with the brushes, too. "You'd beat heavy with two wet mops. Give me those things. Take your sticks back," Oliver finally told him.[10] To please Oliver, Baby learned to play very lightly with the drumsticks and explained why he particularly loved playing on the rims. "I did very little on the wood blocks, more on the shells [the rims of the drums]. They weren't as sharp. The wood blocks gave a tone that was too shrill and sharp for the band. . . . It was up to me to bring out the different expressions for the outfit. If I would be drumming straight and felt that a roll would bring out an expression, I used that. Or If I were playing along and felt that beating the cymbal would help the number, I would do that. It was up to all of us to improve the band . . . and I had to do my part.

"It was my job to study each musician and give a different background for each instrument. When a man is playing it's up to the drummer to give him something to make him feel the music and make him work. . . . At all times I heard every instrument distinctly. I knew when any of them were out of tune or playing the wrong note. I made that a distinct study. Those of us who worked with the King Oliver Band had known each other so long we felt that we were almost related. That outfit had more harmony and feeling of brotherly love than any I ever worked with. And playing music is just like having a home. If you don't have harmony with each other you don't get along. If you've got a family of ten, regardless of what goes on, if you haven't got the harmony you know it's a terrible house. . . . If you haven't got harmony in your band, you haven't got a good band. . . ." Baby recommended a smile in bands where there was no harmony between musicians. "A smile goes a long way,"[11] he advised. He himself had little tussles with Louis Armstrong. Once they ripped each other's silk shirts and went on the bandstand in torn clothes. But their fights were actually friendly, not intended to hurt each other.

While at the Lincoln Gardens, Baby met his second wife, Irene, with whom he lived happily. He bought a car that occasionally landed him in jail for various violations, ranging from assault and battery to reckless driving and speeding and even carrying a dangerous weapon. "All this because I hit [some] fellow's car. I was scared to death," Baby recalled.

"I got a lawyer but he didn't say very much. It cost me almost two hundred dollars to get out of that jam. And still I stayed in jail twenty-four hours and got a record for it."[12]

Baby eventually left Oliver's band when he found out that Oliver was keeping most of the money for recordings the band made, not paying the sidemen properly, Baby said. Soon afterward, in 1925, Baby went to work for his brother in the house band at Burt Kelly's Stables, a cabaret-style nightclub with singing waiters. Kelly didn't like Baby's drumming and ordered him fired. Three years later, Johnny Dodds hired his brother back; Burt Kelly loved Baby's music and didn't even remember the earlier problem.

Baby played in John's group all around town and in other groups, too. He even played at rent parties, at which people charged little fees for food and drink to raise rent money. He kept bumping into Zutty Singleton, who was leading his own group in Chicago at that time. Baby knew all the drummers in Chicago, of course.

"Years later I got [Ben Pollack's] drums through Ray Bauduc," Baby recalled. "I knew Ray from the old days in New Orleans, but he used to come to watch and listen when we were playing at the Three Deuces. I think Pollack owed Ray some money and he gave him the drums in part payment. Bauduc liked my drumming, and he used to ask me how to do various things. . . . Gene Krupa came around for some pointers, too. . . . A lot of white musicians got ideas and pointers from me but I never really taught anyone how to drum."[13]

Baby's biography is a great lesson in the rich jazz history of Chicago. It was one of the leading blues and jazz cities in the country, particularly in the years when Baby lived and played there. The musicians he played with were among the leading lights of the time. Few of them, with the exception of Louis Armstrong, ever became wealthy from playing jazz. Even Gene Krupa had his ups and downs and had to contend with a scandal that injured his reputation and affected his career. But like Baby, all the early drummers left a priceless legacy.

CHAPTER

MORE ABOUT THE EARLY JAZZ DRUMMERS

FOUR

Many excellent drummers began their careers in the 1920s. Some would go on to modernize their playing and become so versatile that they would hold impressive jobs in groups in both the swing and bebop eras and beyond. Some, such as Buddy Rich, led groups into the 1980s. The next section discusses some of the lesser-known drummers, who had important, successful careers in their era.

PART ONE
THE LESSER-KNOWN EARLY JAZZ AND SWING-ERA DRUMMERS

George Wettling, who was born in Topeka, Kansas, in 1907, grew up in Chicago. He began playing professionally with big bands in 1924, and may have played with the Wolverines, a leading white group known for New Orleans-rooted, Chicago-style music. Wettling, mightily influenced by Baby Dodds, always played with a four-beats-to-the-bar bass drum style; Wettling also added color and shadings, and he had a delicate touch for his firm, supple feeling for time.

Wettling played with great ease in small groups and big bands. The names of the leaders he played with reads like a Who's Who of swing-era jazz from the 1930s on. They include clarinetist Artie Shaw, guitarist Eddie Condon, saxophonist Charlie Barnet, clarinetist Woody Herman, and Paul Whiteman, who called himself the King of Jazz.

Drummer **Ben Pollack**, who had a good reputation in the 1920s and 1930s, was very much influenced by Zutty Singleton and Baby Dodds, too. Early in his career, Pollack, who had been born in Chicago in 1903, played with the New Orleans Rhythm Kings, a white group in Chicago,

George Wettling

and established himself as a leading drummer. By 1926, he was leading his own jazz-influenced dance bands, and he hired youthful musicians destined for fame and fortune—Benny Goodman, Glenn Miller, Bud Freeman, Jack Teagarden, Harry James, Muggsy Spanier—and drummer Gene Krupa at the start of his career. Pollack can be seen in action to this day in the movie entitled *The Glenn Miller Story.*

In WKCR's radio series about the history of jazz drums, Mel Lewis and Loren Schoenberg included a 1928 recording by Ben Pollack. Lewis admired his innovative cymbal technique. "He played a lot of cymbals," Mel said, noting how Pollack rode—kept time—on the Chinese cymbal, and then later on rode out on it, too. "And he played a lot of nice things on four," Mel said. "He was heavier [a better drummer] than I thought. And everyone [in the recording studio] rushing, and everyone frantic, and he was probably pushed back thirty feet in the corner someplace. A lot of the old-timers [in a band] had a tendency to rush, and the drummer tried to hold them back."[1] Mel also admired Pollack's fills—improvisations—and thought they had much in common with the work of the great drummer Sonny Greer in Duke Ellington's band from the late 1920s until the early 1950s.

Kaiser Marshall played drums with Fletcher Henderson's band in the 1920s. He went on to play and record with other well-known musicians of the era, including Louis Armstrong, with whom he recorded "Knockin' a Jug."

Another good drummer in the 1930s, *George Stafford*, who was based in New York, didn't have a national reputation. Bandleader Luis Russell, born in Panama and raised in New Orleans, hired New Orleans-born, pioneering drummer **Paul Barbarin**, with a subtle, simple, but much-admired style. Barbarin, using press rolls, knew how to hit a groove and maintain it—that is, to keep swinging with a happy, deep feeling. "He didn't do much except swing, and that's all you have to do," Mel Lewis observed about Barbarin. "Barbarin played with Louis Armstrong on records, too. These guys did marvelous things and contributed to the art form."[2]

Mel Lewis's father had been a drummer in Buffalo, New York, so Lewis grew up in a drum-loving household. What he didn't know from his own experience, he undoubtedly learned from talking to his father and his father's friends. And so Mel was able to pass on some of the legend and lore about the earlier drummers, such as **Stan King**—someone rarely cited as an important jazz drummer. King had a drinking problem, yet maintained his position as a top studio man in the 1920s and early 1930s. "The amazing thing was how many record dates he got [despite] his problem. The Dorsey brothers [Tommy and Jimmy, leading bandleaders of the swing era] were nuts about him," said Lewis.[3]

Ray Bauduc, a white drummer born in New Orleans in 1909, grew up in the traditions of his hometown and was strongly influenced by

Ray Bauduc

both Baby Dodds and Zutty Singleton. In 1928, when Ray became a member of Ben Pollack's band, he began to establish his own style combining vaudeville, ragtime, and basic New Orleans rhythms. After leaving Pollack's band, Bauduc joined Bob Crosby and the Bobcats. Bob Crosby (singer Bing's brother) had a wonderful band rooted in New Orleans music. With the Bobcats, Ray Bauduc became part of jazz's legend and lore as a fiery soloist and exciting showman.

He is particularly remembered for his recording of "Big Noise From Winnetka," a hit song on which he played a duet with bassist Bob Haggart. With his sticks, Bauduc played his drum solo on the strings of the bass, while Haggart did the fingering! The sound was astounding, brash, and exciting. One young bassist listening to the record was so impressed that he taught himself to get the same sound by flicking his fingers across the strings. Not until much later did he learn the recording was really of a duet![4]

Like Northern drummers, Bauduc also used his sticks on the bass drum and the rims of the snare and bass drums. He also used two small tom-toms on the bass drum and may have invented a pedal tom-tom.[5] He won a *Down Beat* magazine award for drummers in 1940. After leaving the Bobcats in 1942, Bauduc played with famous swing-era bandleaders including trombonist Tommy Dorsey, Benny Goodman, violinist Joe Venuti, trombonist Jack Teagarden, and then saxophonist Jimmy Dorsey, Tommy's brother.

Jimmy Crawford played drums with a famed African-American, swing-era band led by Jimmy Lunceford. Crawford's strong, solid pulsation was a trademark of Lunceford's sound. Crawford provided great support for that band, playing heavily when necessary, lightly when the music called for that sort of touch, and always reliably. After spending fourteen years with Lunceford, in 1943 Crawford moved on to other groups—tenor saxophonist Ben Webster's, then clarinetist Edmond Hall's at New York's Café Society. Located in Greenwich Village, it was New York City's first racially integrated downtown club.

Then Crawford played in the highly respected band of Fletcher Henderson, whose arrangements were prized by such white bandleaders as Benny Goodman, and with trumpeter Harry James, and with the progressive jazz orchestra leader Stan Kenton. After the big-band era ended, versatile Crawford played in Broadway orchestras for musical comedies and recorded with many more prominent bandleaders and singers.

Ray McKinley, basically a rhythm drummer, not a soloist, could swing and uplift a group effortlessly. He played with the forty-piece Glenn Miller Army Air Force Band in 1943, using drums and cymbals imaginatively—but not for the purpose of showing off in an era when drum soloists were very popular. The Miller band, which became legendary itself, numbered among McKinley's high-profile jobs.

Born in Fort Worth, Texas, on June 10, 1910, he began playing as a child and essentially taught himself about drumming. He left town to travel with respected regional bands in the Southwest. In 1927, having reached Chicago, he was sitting in with Ben Pollack's band in a club called the Blackhawk when he met a struggling young trombonist named Glenn Miller. Their friendship led McKinley to play with Miller's band.

McKinley thought the Pollack band sounded terrific. Six months later, Pollack returned the compliment by hiring McKinley as a second drummer for the group. But a great trombonist, Jack Teagarden, went into the band around that time and brought drummer Ray Bauduc with him. So McKinley lost out that time. But he found other jobs. Bassist Bob Haggart noticed how much McKinley's playing developed in this period.

McKinley was very impressed with the way drummer Walter Johnson, with Fletcher Henderson's band, and Chick Webb, with his own band, played the hi-hat in the early 1930s. From Chick in particular, McKinley learned to play the hi-hat. McKinley said about himself: "I went with the flow," about the hi hat, as well as about playing straight 4/4 time. "I had to."[6] "[McKinley] manipulated the 'hat' with his hands and sticks in a very provocative and swinging way; he played a bunch of variations on the basic dotted eighth and sixteenth rhythm and really got the band moving. McKinley used the hi-hat as an instrument in itself," explained Mel Lewis.[7]

With Glenn Miller, who wrote arrangements, and a few more friends who had played in another regional band, McKinley joined the Dorsey Brothers Orchestra in 1934. He stayed with it until the brothers had a big fight in a club, the Glen Island Casino, in the summer of 1935. Tommy walked away from the band, and Jimmy took it over. McKinley stayed with it. Through all the ups and downs of his career, McKinley was known as a thoughtful performer who kept his timekeeping duties uppermost in his mind. He used a varied drum set—the bass drum, the snare, woodblock, rims, the hi-hat, a cowbell, tom-toms, and cymbals—and stuck to the slower, two-beat feeling of New Orleans music.

With the less-distinguished Jimmy Dorsey band, McKinley kept working hard. Many bandleaders, including Tommy Dorsey, sought McKinley to play for them, but he stayed with Jimmy Dorsey out of friendship. McKinley was always noted for his affectionate personality. He declared himself to be unambitious; perhaps that's why he never felt he had to become a fully modernized swing drummer. But he retained his easy, attractive qualities, and he was ambitious enough to love some of the classiest swing-era drummers in jazz—not only Chick Webb and Walter Johnson, but Davey Tough in his days with Woody Herman's First Herd, Gene Krupa when he played with Benny Goodman, and perhaps the most important drummer of all, Papa Jo Jones.

Lesser known but fascinating to McKinley was his contemporary Ray Bauduc, plus the younger drummers Shelly Manne, Jack Sperling, Nick Fatool (whose work can be heard on recordings with studio bands and with Louis Armstrong), and Louie Bellson, a white drummer who played with Duke Ellington for a while before integrated bands were taken more or less for granted. (In the South, Bellson, with his dark hair, sat in the back of Duke's orchestra and didn't call attention to himself. So he got by.)

McKinley would keep his mind open to all the styles and positive aspects of innovations in drumming to come. He would admire the better rock drummers for their new ideas for the bass drum—and their occasional use of two bass drums—and for their vitality that attracted fans. But like Mel Lewis, McKinley noticed that rock drummers had problems playing straight-ahead, simple time—four to the bar, for example. And he was very amused by their huge drum sets, which they sometimes set up primarily as a spectacle.

In 1939, he formed a band himself with Will Bradley, under Bradley's name. They had quite a bit of success with a boogie-woogie style, featuring McKinley's drumming and singing. One of their big hits was a tune in 1940 called "The Celery Stalks at Midnight," on which McKinley sang about a stalk of celery walking down the highway.

He played with Jerry Gray, sharing leadership of that dance band after Glenn Miller was lost in an airplane in wartime Europe. Later, McKinley led his own band. In 1947, he made some recordings of harmonically advanced-sounding arrangements written by noted arranger Eddie Sauter. McKinley organized a new Glenn Miller Orchestra, which performed the classic Miller repertory and toured the world from 1956 to 1966. Afterward, McKinley led his own big band, then a small group, and in 1973 took over from bandleader Tex Beneke and led that band until 1978. McKinley lived a long life and enjoyed a successful career crowned with the respect and affection of other musicians.

J. C. Heard, born in Dayton, Ohio, on October 8, 1917, began his career as a dancer, as many drummers did, and started playing drums as a teenager. (This drummer is not to be confused with the contemporary bassist named J. C. Heard born in 1938.) In his early twenties, drummer Heard moved to New York and played with the popular pianist Teddy Wilson, who had his own band. He began working with many of the era's best-known musicians—multi-talented horn player, bandleader, arranger, and composer Benny Carter, soulful saxophonist and singer Louis Jordan, Count Basie, Louis Armstrong, tenor saxophonist Coleman Hawkins (known as King of the Tenor Saxophone), and Cab Calloway. In 1946, Heard received *Esquire* magazine's Drummer of the Year award and went on to play in 1948 with pianist Erroll Garner, the composer of "Misty."

Heard played with important bebop groups, led one himself, and toured in the Far East and Europe, then moved to Detroit, Michigan, where he led his own groups beginning in the mid-1960s. His style owed much to more famous drummers whom he most admired, Papa Jo Jones and Big Sid Catlett.

PART TWO
THE MASTERFUL
SWING-ERA DRUMMERS

The early master drummers, who began playing in the 1920s when Chicago was the center of the jazz world, included the following men.

Davey Tough, the son of Scottish immigrants, was born in Oak Park, Illinois, in 1907. By the time he was sixteen, he was playing drums with the musical Austin High School Gang and becoming known for his lifestyle as a very talented, bohemian-style musician and writer. He frequented poetry readings and art museums. He also earned a reputation as a very heavy drinker.

Until 1927, he played with the Chicago Wolverines. That year, he married, went to Europe with his wife and a clarinetist, and worked with various bands in France, Belgium, and Germany. In Europe, Tough hung out with Britain's Prince of Wales, who sat in to play Tough's drums. Tough read *The Sun Also Rises* by Ernest Heminway, the new star among novelists. And Tough drank and drank. When he went back to Chicago, he spent most of his time drinking. Other musicians saw him looking ragged and hanging out with bums in the streets. He was a tiny man, very short and weighing only about 100 pounds (45.36 kg).

But Tough maintained his stature as a very talented drummer. He moved on to New York and frequented the little wall-to-wall jazz clubs on West 52nd Street, which later became known as Swing Street. Sitting in at those clubs, he did a brilliant job at accompanying. Because of his drinking, however, he was too unreliable to hold down a steady job in a band.

When Gene Krupa left Benny Goodman's band in 1938, Goodman took the chance of hiring Tough, who distinguished himself there for a short time. Davey played with looseness, simplicity, and great drive. Having studied the styles of Zutty and Baby attentively, Davey had gone on to inspire the Chicago players with both rhythmic drive and subtlety. He was particularly known for his swing. But Goodman had to let Davey go from the band because he had too many collapses and disappearances caused by drinking. His first marriage ended in divorce at this time.

Tommy Dorsey, the trombonist, starting his own band in 1936, gambled on Davey, who managed to hold on to his job for two years and gave the band "a fresh and buoyant feeling."[8] Davey also started writing a witty column on drumming for *Metronome*, a popular jazz magazine. By 1938, because of his drinking problem, Davey was roaming around in the big-band world, moving from the Dorsey band to Bunny Berigan, back to Dorsey, to Benny Goodman, on to Bud Freeman, and then to Joe Marsala on 52nd Street. Davey sojourned with clarinetist Artie Shaw's very popular band, played for Woody Herman and for Charlie Spivak's band in 1942, then joined Artie Shaw's Navy Band.

Artie knew Davey as an alcoholic who could always find something to drink. Occasionally he fell off bandstands. Artie had to assign someone to keep an eye on him on performance days. But about Davey's drumming, Artie Shaw told jazz critic Whitney Balliett, "I think he was the most underrated band drummer in jazz, and he got a beautiful sound out of his instrument. He tuned his drums, he tried to achieve on them what he heard in his head. . . . He refused to take solos. Whenever I pointed to him for twelve or eight or four bars, he'd smile and shake his head and go on playing rhythm drums."[9]

One of the best-known parts of Davey's career was yet to come. In 1944, he married Casey Majors, an African-American woman whom he had met in Philadelphia.[10] And he joined Woody Herman's exciting young band called Herman's Herd, a hard-swinging, big jazz band. Davey Tough won critics' polls in music magazines. He retained traces of his New Orleans drum-style past, but for the most part he heralded the new style to come. He kept time on the cymbal, with each beat melding into the next one, so that he seemed to be playing long lines.

He kept his drum heads tuned loosely, and that way he got a dull sound instead of a loud boom. Other drummers joked that his drum heads flapped. And he used many bass drum offbeats—dropping bombs, in effect. On slow tempos, he implied double time by halving the notes, thus giving the tempo a vital lift. Every modern drummer would begin to use the same device.

Bassist Chubby Jackson paid attention to all the tasteful things that Davey did for the band to make it sound bigger or speedier and brighter. "[H]e'd hit five quarter notes in a row as a signal to the boys to pep up. He was the little general of that first Herman's Herd," Jackson said. Davey doctored his cymbals to get particular sounds, and he adjusted his approach behind every soloist, "playing a ride cymbal behind a clarinetist, and a Chinese cymbal behind a trombone, and a tightly closing high hat (sic) with clicking afterbeats struck on the high hat post with one stick behind a piano," and more ideas for other players.[11]

Davey controlled his drinking to a degree, but it got the better of him in September 1945. He left Herman's band and wandered from group to group, all of them excellent, in New York and Chicago. In 1948, he spent several months in a hospital. Drunk one night, on the way home to his wife, he fell down and fractured his skull. He died in a hospital the next day.

William Alexander "Sonny" Greer, a singing drummer, would become famous for his part in helping to establish Duke Ellington's band and embellishing Duke's original compositions. Greer could take the bare bones of an idea from Ellington and develop it into a tasteful work of art. That was the responsibility of the great drummers and their relationship to arrangements for the big bands. Greer acquitted himself with royal aplomb.

He was born in Long Branch, New Jersey, maybe as early as 1895 (though he sometimes said 1902 and other years). He taught himself to play drums, and his primary influence was a vaudeville drummer who gave him advice about music and showmanship. In return, Sonny taught the drummer how to play pool.[12] It was a time when showmanship for drummers was very important, and it was not enough for a drummer simply to play well. Greer moved to Washington where he met Ellington around 1920.

Sonny Greer with Ellington's Band

A few years older than Ellington, Greer was in his twenties and was already a polished showman, a hipster, a wit, and a storyteller. He immediately became friends with the elegant, gifted Duke, whose father had worked on the White House's household staff. Duke and Sonny played together in a band Duke led at the Howard Theater, an important theater for African-American performers touring major cities. Greer began talking about the glories of New York to Duke and their buddies—other budding musicians Duke already had in his early band, which worked steadily in the Washington area.

When a leader asked Greer to play drums in a band in New York, Greer also got the leader to hire Duke and another buddy or two. At first Duke hesitated; he had established a career as a dance-band leader in Washington. But he couldn't resist the glamorous image of Harlem. He, Sonny, and their friends took jobs as sidemen in New York. But something may have gone wrong with that job. Either it didn't materialize when the men reached New York, or when the band there was scheduled to go on tour, the sidemen decided to stay in New York and try to build careers. They quickly sank to the level of hustling pool for a few dollars to get money to eat. Luckily for them, Sonny was a good pool player.

Duke went back to Washington and the sweet smell of biscuits and plentiful food in his mother's house. Then Sonny and other musicians lured him back to New York with the promise of another job. That fell through, and the fellows were briefly back to hustling. But Duke began to make his way by playing piano as a sideman in a basement dive near Times Square for four years. Sonny was in the group, too. It wasn't Duke's band yet, but it turned into that. He began hiring many of the musicians, including Sonny, who would go with him into the Cotton Club. When it had a vacancy for a band in 1927, Ellington and his ten-man orchestra auditioned and were hired.

Gangsters owned the Cotton Club, which had a whites-only policy for its audience. But on the bright side, it provided Ellington with a stable forum from which to launch himself as a bandleader, composer, and orchestrator. His creativity blossomed. And Greer's part in the band became legendary.

Sometimes Greer shared announcing duties with Duke. Greer sang such songs as "Dinah." "Send me, man!" Greer would shout as he launched a percussion volley.[13] He and Duke's bandsinger, Ivie Anderson, who had grown up in an orphanage, had a very close professional relationship; they played duets that charmed audiences. He would try to help her as he watched her go through asthma attacks backstage. She left the band in the late 1940s, retiring because of her health. Sonny refused to play duets with any other bandsingers.

Greer had an elaborate drum set that attracted the envious stares of other drummers. He estimated its value at $3,000; it was built for him by the Leedy Company.[14] In the early 1950s, popular and highly respected, Greer left the band, but he continued to play, primarily as a rhythm drummer and a showman, for the rest of his life. He died in New York in 1982. For his dramatic and showmanlike timekeeping work and the artful fills he did for Duke's band, Greer earned the reputation of being one of the very important drummers in jazz history.

William "Cozy" Cole, born in East Orange, New Jersey, in the first decade of the twentieth century, started playing drums at an early age,

Cozy Cole

perhaps five, and a few years later had the drum seat in his school band. He was so in love with drums that he became Sonny Greer's band boy, carrying his drums around, when both young hopefuls were living in New Jersey.

For a while, Cozy helped support his brothers, a sister, and a paternal grandmother by doing a number of jobs ranging from housework to dancing. But he couldn't resist taking lessons from a professional drummer at Harlem's Lafayette Theater.

One of his early jobs as a professional was probably with the band of Wilbur Sweatman (the same bandleader who gave Ellington his first job in New York). After that gig, Cozy Cole tried leading his own group. He recorded "Load of Coal" with pianist Jelly Roll Morton on the Victor label in 1930 and then, in the 1930s, played in groups led by singer Blanche Calloway (Cab Calloway's sister), sax player Benny Carter, and violinist Stuff Smith, with whom Cole worked on 52nd Street.

He studied constantly, taking lessons to play the timpani from Saul Goodman of the New York Philharmonic. Cole became prominent during his four years with Cab Calloway's band, from 1938 to 1942, taking part in Calloway's great recordings of that period. Two were called "Paradiddle" and "Ratamacue," named for a couple of the rudiments of drum playing. Another was called "Crescendo in Drums."

In the 1940s, he studied music at Juilliard School in New York — though it had no jazz department. He also led his own groups and toured and recorded with Louis Armstrong's All Stars, the small group that made a hit in a New York concert. That convinced the trumpeter to lead a small group instead of a big band for the rest of his life. (Cole followed Satchmo's favorite drummer, Big Sid Catlett, into that group.) Cole also co-owned a drum school with Gene Krupa in the 1950s and 1960s and appeared in several well-known movies, such as *Make Mine Music* and *The Glenn Miller Story* — the latter often appears on television. Cozy was one of the first African-Americans to perform on film soundtracks, play on the staff at CBS Radio, and work for bandleaders such as Benny Goodman.

Cole's recording of "Topsy" in 1958 with his own group was a hit — a gold record with sales of half a million copies. He remained a leader throughout the 1960s. In 1969, he joined trumpeter Jonah Jones's very popular small group and worked freelance, in much demand, into the 1970s. He died in 1981. Until the last moment, he was still studying and lecturing at Ohio's Capitol University.[15]

William Henry "Chick" Webb, who was born on February 10, 1909, was a phenomenon — a ground-breaking drummer as a musician, a soloist, and a showman. He had a highly respected big band based in Harlem beginning in the late 1920s, before he was twenty years old. Other bandleaders admired Chick Webb's group so much that they frequently raided the personnel and hired excellent players away from him.

Chick hadn't really wanted to lead his own band. He was a hunchback, possibly or at least in part as the result of a childhood accident. And he was so diminutive that he was probably a dwarf. But Duke Ellington encouraged Chick to lead, and the result was a splendid band. Chick led the house band at the Savoy Ballroom in Harlem beginning in 1928, after the managers of that second-floor walk-up ballroom, so popular with dancers, heard Chick's band successfully compete against bands led by Fletcher Henderson and King Oliver.

Nearly ten years later, drummer Gene Krupa also felt the sting of defeat when the Benny Goodman band went into competition with Chick's at the Savoy. Krupa later wrote about his historic encounter: "I'll never forget that night, the night when Benny's band battled Chick at the Savoy — he just cut me to ribbons — made me feel awfully small . . . that man was dynamic; he could reach the most amazing heights. When he really let go, you had the feeling that the entire atmosphere in the place was being charged. When he felt like it, he could cut down any of us."[16]

Chick is best remembered these days for the girl singer he hired in the mid-1920s — Ella Fitzgerald, with whom he had major hits such as "A Tisket, A Tasket." But in his own time, other musicians studied his style and hoped to play half as well as he did.

Chick Webb

Everyone wondered where Chick's strength and energy came from. All the drummers marveled at and learned from his crackling recording of "Liza." He appeared on the cover of the Gretsch drum catalog; he was that prominent drum company's top man, with his totally customized drum set. The set had to be specially built for him, because of his physical handicaps. For one thing, his feet couldn't reach the bass drum pedal. And his drums were set up on racks, an innovation in the early 1930s.

On the WKCR radio show, Mel Lewis and Loren Schoenberg played a recording of "Don't Be That Way," written by Chick's lead alto saxophonist and arranger, Edgar Sampson. Chick played brushes all the way through, and he had to hit his cymbals hard; he crashed them, and he was swinging all the way. It was unheard of in those days, Mel said, for anyone to play brushes on an uptempo swinger. Chick Webb did it. He was a flamboyant showman and the first true jazz drum soloist, a major influence on other drummers—Gene Krupa in particular. Because Chick led his own band, he could give himself the leeway to take as much time in the spotlight as he wanted. His influence was directly responsible for Krupa's work on tom-toms for "Sing Sing Sing" at Carnegie Hall. (That influence came from Baby Dodds and Zutty Singleton on tom-toms first and from Chick, too.) And then master drummer Buddy Rich emerged at the time and did what Gene did, "and twice as fast," Mel Lewis noticed. "So Buddy was out of Chick, too."[17]

Chick contracted spinal tuberculosis. He kept working, even though he was always in terrible pain. Finally, he had to go to the hospital in Baltimore for treatments. When they didn't work, and he knew that he was dying, he asked his mother to help him sit up in bed. There's a legend that he looked at the people, including band members, gathered around him and said, "Sorry, fellows, but I've got to go.' And he died in 1939.

Big Sid Catlett began playing in the early swing era and became one of the most popular drummers for bebop groups. He was more of a journeyman than a virtuoso, but he was so reliable on the bandstand and so affable in his private life that he couldn't help but succeed in the jazz field. (People are often asked to play in groups because of their good relationships with other musicians.) Of course most of all, in Catlett's case, he succeeded because of his virtuosity.

Born on January 17, 1910, in Evansville, Indiana, a suburb of Chicago, where he had some music lessons as a child, he soon moved to Chicago. He taught himself to play by listening attentively to drummer Zutty Sin-

gleton. Big Sid even asked to sit in at the clubs where Zutty was playing with Armstrong. By age nineteen, Sid began a succession of jobs
with excellent big bands.

Sid led his own groups from 1944 to 1946. Both before and after
that, he played in Armstrong's groups, the big band in the 1930s and the
small group called the All-Stars in the 1940s; he was Satchmo's favorite
drummer.

Sid always asked the other musicians in a group what they wanted
him to play. Brushes? Sticks on the Chinese cymbal? Anything they
wanted, he played for them; adaptability was a hallmark of his style.
Pianist Earl Hines viewed Catlett as a great soloist and a great accompanist. He never overwhelmed the sound of the people he was playing
with, and he had an uncanny ability to anticipate what a man would play
in his solo and embellish that.

"His library of accompanying techniques was endless," critic Whitney Balliett wrote. "He used different cymbals behind different instruments—a heavy ride cymbal behind a trumpet; the high hat *(sic)*, its
cymbals half closed, behind a trombone; a Chinese cymbal, with its siz-
zling sound, behind a clarinet. All the while his left hand worked out an
extraordinary series of accents on the snare drum. . . . Catlett was
supremely subtle. He implied more than he stated in his background
work, yet he controlled every performance. He told [trumpeter] Ruby
Braff he could swing seventeen men with a single wire brush and a tele-
phone book to play it on, and he was right. He reined in the obstreper-
ous, pushed the laggardly, and celebrated the inspired. His taste was
faultless, his time was perfect [most drummers, no matter how profi-
cient, play a split second behind the beat, but Catlett was purposely a
split second ahead], and the sound he got on his drums was handsome,
careful, and rich."[18]

"Catlett was a master at brushes," emphasized modern drummer
Kenny Washington, an authority on drumming history. "He had 17
different ways of playing brushes."[19] And that was just one aspect of
his mastery.

Sid Catlett with singer Billie Holiday

Catlett's solos were varied and imaginative, and he had a great control of his stage presence, so that he could play slick games with his sticks. At about 6 feet 3 inches (190.5 cm), and of massive proportions, he made a dramatic spectacle. His games with the sticks — he sometimes threw them up in the air and dropped them for effect — aggravated Benny Goodman, because Big Sid had all eyes in the audience focused on him when he played with the Goodman band. Sid left the band after that. The talk was that Goodman didn't like the competition. But other leaders didn't mind sharing the spotlight with the charming, virtuosic drummer. "Catlett could do it all," says Kenny Washington.[20]

Catlett was also famous for his relentless rounds of clubs—and every place else in any town he worked in. He loved to socialize with musicians and listen to them play; he loved to gamble and to be in the company of women. He hated to stay home and miss anything. It wasn't surprising that he had a heart attack in 1949 and had to leave Armstrong's group. Armstrong's manager sent Sid to the mountains for a rest, but he didn't stay there long. He moved between New York and Chicago for the next two years, working and sitting in for pleasure in clubs. One night, visiting a friend backstage in a Chicago theater, he collapsed and died at age forty-one.

Gene Krupa, a showman and fiery drummer, was born into a large, poor family in Chicago on January 15, 1900. He began to attract attention on recordings made with guitarist Eddie Condon in Chicago in the 1920s. As soon as Gene started out to become a professional drummer, he noticed that gifted African-American drummers were the pacesetters and innovators. Though he knew excellent white drummers, he learned primarily from the African-Americans, from their "seemingly endless flow of ideas and energy" and "freedom."[21] Gene learned about the tradition of the blues, from which jazz had evolved.

Gene spent several years moving around, learning from Chick Webb and other musicians in Harlem and playing in the studios. Eventually he got a chance to join Benny Goodman's group in 1934. It was with Goodman that Gene really distinguished himself in 1938 at the Carnegie Hall jazz concert. But Benny couldn't tolerate how much attention Krupa won for his performance on tom-toms for "Sing Sing Sing." Though their duet was one of the highlights of the concert, Krupa and Benny soon argued so fiercely that Krupa left to lead his own band in April 1938. He and Goodman maintained great respect for each other, however.

Gene's band got off to a good start, with guest appearances on Tommy Dorsey's radio show and recordings for the Brunswick company. Gene had excellent players in his band. Its recording of "Drum Boogie" turned out to be one of its most popular numbers. His band singer, Irene Daye, left and was replaced by Anita O'Day, one of the best, most swinging, and hippest jazz singers who ever lived. Then Gene hired Roy Eldridge, an equally hip trumpeter. With Anita and Roy, an African-American trumpet star, singing duets in the band, Gene led some classic

Gene Krupa with singer Anita O'Day

recordings, particularly with the tunes "Let Me Off Uptown" and "Knock Me a Kiss." With Eldridge, Gene had more hits with the instrumentals "After You've Gone" and "Rockin' Chair."

Gene was the first drummer to use the bass drum to record in studios. Overriding the recording engineers, who were afraid of any drums and muffled them in the early days, Krupa insisted on playing the bass drum—and he had the courage to assert himself even in the days before he became a big name. There were a lot of arguments between drummers and engineers in the recording studios in the early days. Krupa won and helped open the door for other drummers.

Baby Dodds had noticed young Gene in the audiences, taking lessons by ear. Gene, despite his big ego, was always willing to give credit where it was due; he often talked about Chick's influence. He called drummers such as Baby and Chick the masters and himself their student.

Gene eventually talked about his attention to all aspects of music, not just the drum's role in a group—"not just pure, plain driving rhythm. I try to produce sounds that blend with what's going on."[22]

He explained to writer George T. Simon about the different sounds and nuances of the cymbals, depending upon where they were hit. "Drum solos must have substance and continuity. Before I begin one, I try to have a good idea of what I'm going to play. Then, while I'm playing, I'll hum some sort of thing to myself, something maybe like 'boom-did-dee, boom-did-dee, boom-did-dee, boom' and follow that with another phrase that relates to the one I've just played. At the same time I keep on humming to myself so that each syllable becomes not only a separate beat but also a separate sound. That's very imortant, because drums, if they're to be musical, must produce sounds, not just noise. So a 'boom' could be a deep-sounding tom-tom, and a 'dang' a rim shot, and a 'paaah' could be a thin cymbal."[23]

Gene had the bad luck to be arrested in California in 1943 on a charge of possessing marijuana. Various versions of the story circulated. Gene was quoted as saying he actually didn't like marijuana and preferred alcohol. But a valet who was going away to the army bought him marijuana for a present. The gift turned out to be Gene's going-away present, too—he went away to jail. The valet may have told the wrong people about the gift; someone alerted the police, and they arrested Gene. For the original charge, a misdemeanor, Gene spent ninety days in jail. But the case achieved great notoriety; Gene was accused of being responsible for increasing juvenile delinquency in the country, because his valet was a minor.

So Gene had to face another trial relating to juvenile delinquency. Gene lost that case, too, and spent eighty-four days in jail on a felony conviction. When he got out, he discovered that all his friends had disappeared. Only his ex-wife was waiting to see him. The flamboyance of his stage performances had done nothing to make him seem innocent.

But in the music world, Krupa was destined to remain popular. Benny Goodman called and offered him a job. Gene took it gratefully. About two months later, he went to work with the Tommy Dorsey Band. When he opened with Dorsey at the famed Paramount Theater in New York, audiences cheered him wildly. Gene was overcome with emotion and gave flowery speeches of thanks. Eventually the felony conviction in California was overturned.

He continued to lead groups—some musically excellent, some commercially oriented. He always felt proud to be able to attract people to jazz and win respect and financial rewards for drummers. He never made the transition to a more modern, bebop style in the 1940s. Although he tried to make little adjustments for bebop, he always remained a swing drummer, playing the pulse on the snare drum, the bass drum, and the hi-hat cymbal. He never switched over to keep time on the ride cymbals, nor did he use the bass drum sparingly for accents or "bombs" or feather it subtly. He had contracted a happy marriage with the snare drum in the swing era, and that is what he remained loyal to.

He spent some pleasant years in the 1950s touring with an important jazz concert series called Jazz at the Philharmonic, but he began to slow down with age. Late in his career, he performed in a club, the Metropole, on Broadway near Times Square. It was a far cry from Carnegie Hall.

His last years were particularly difficult. He had a heart attack in the mid-1960s; he also developed emphysema, ruptured spinal disks, and leukemia. He and his second wife were divorced, and he suffered from the separation from his two children.[24]

In the summer of 1973, he was given an award by his fellow drummers during a Newport Jazz Festival in New York. "He looked terribly tired. Walking was extremely difficult," George T. Simon remembered about Gene on that day. He was living in an apartment badly damaged by fire in Yonkers, New York. Only the kitchen was livable. In October 1973, Gene died. Simon, who gave the eulogy at the funeral, commented, "I couldn't have spoken for a nicer guy."[25]

Buddy Rich, a great, fiery drummer, was called a genius and a superdrummer by some drummers, including Gene Krupa, and a lightweight by others, who claimed Buddy didn't do anything innovative on the drums. All he did was create exceptional excitement, they said[26]—as if that wasn't enough.

He began working as a dancer, singer, and drummer in his family's vaudeville act, Wilson and Rich, when he was so young that he couldn't remember the start of his career clearly. By the 1930s, after he had already been playing the drums for years, he decided to commit himself to playing jazz drums. That was after he had already been earning $1,000 a week as a kid star, he said, traveling on the road with his father and a tutor in 1932. That's one version of the story. Buddy also said that he told his father he wanted to join the musicians' union in New York and become a jazz drummer. His father gave him the $54 needed for the union's fee. Buddy had no job at the time. So all the money he had earned as a child apparently was gone.

He lived with his family in Sheepshead Bay, Brooklyn, in a home he described as warm and happy. Finding a job with Joe Marsala's band for $46 a week, Buddy kept $10 and gave his father the rest. "Marsala told me just to play with woodblocks (*sic*) and a sizzle cymbal and no high hat (*sic*) and a lot of ricky-tick stuff on the rims. But gradually I brought in other equipment and we moved over to a four-four beat," Buddy reminisced about his development for jazz writer Whitney Balliett.[27]

He began to move around the big band scene, playing with Bunny Berigan, then Tommy Dorsey. Buddy didn't get along with Dorsey at all.

Not even a broken arm could stop drummer Buddy Rich, here with singer Jane Harvey (left) and bandleader Alvy West (right).

Dorsey once told someone that Buddy was as awful as Hitler.[28] Then Buddy formed his own band in 1946, at the end of the big-band era, when all the bands were breaking up. He was backed by funds from Frank Sinatra, he said. In two years, the band went broke. But it was a swinging band, he remembered proudly.

In the 1950s, he worked with Norman Granz's Jazz at the Philharmonic series with some of the biggest and best stars in jazz. (Gene Krupa would say he suffered by comparison to Buddy on those Jazz at the Philharmonic tours.) He then formed his own small band and worked with trumpeter Harry James for a while, but he never felt satisfied without a big band.

He was only forty-two years old when, in 1959, he had a heart attack as he was leading a small group in a New Orleans club. He didn't know what had hit him. He thought a bath would cure him, but he ended up spending time in an oxygen tent and then months in a hospital. He was told he should never play drums again. For a month he did nothing but sit at home, but he couldn't stand the boredom. So he went back to work as a singer. Audiences wanted him to play, however, and he began again—and had another heart attack, this time as he was playing golf in Las Vegas with a friend, the popular singer Billy Eckstine.

"Who knows why?" Buddy told Whitney Balliett. "I was told it was twenty years of anxiety, temperament, and unhappiness. And I used to have terrible eating habits—three pounds [1.36 kg] of spaghetti at four in the morning after work and then go to bed." He realized his lifestyle was killing him. He also knew he should never get excited, because he had such a terrible temper.[29]

But he didn't let his heart condition force him to quit working, and somehow he survived for a long time, organizing a big band in 1966 and playing with it until the mid-1970s. He then played mainly in New York, where he owned a popular jazz club, Buddy's Place. In the 1980s, he toured with a band of young musicians.

He talked about his masterful drum style to Whitney Balliett. "Maybe my technique is greased elbows, and maybe it's because the Man Upstairs talked to my hands and said 'be fast' and they were." Buddy never practiced, and he never had a lesson in his life, he said. "All these guys get from practicing is tired wrists. If you have something to play, you hear it in your heart and mind, and then you go and try it out in front of an audience. I read a little drum music, but an arranger can't write for a drummer. Only the drummer knows where the fills and the accents go. When we get a new arrangement, I don't play it. I sit out front and listen. Then I play it once and that's it. I don't see anything in my mind when I solo. I'm not trying to play clichés. I tell myself, 'Make sure you don't play anything you played last night.' Playing a drum solo is like telling a story. It has a beginning, a middle, and . . . a punch line."[30]

He said that with his drumming he told people about his wife, his daughter, and the other nice people he was with before he got on the bandstand. The sight of Johnny Carson, the witty television talk-show host, made Buddy try to play in a light, funny way. When he saw Count Basie, he played with love in his heart. Sometimes people told him he sounded vicious, and Buddy thought he might have been thinking about thirty years of one-nighters and the drag of his stint in the Marines, when he had gotten into fights with people who insulted Jews.

"But the next night I'll go where I'm playing and say, 'Sorry little drums, I'll be tender tonight.' Drums can be as musical as [legendary violinist Jascha] Heifetz. You don't pick up sticks as if they were hammers. It's a matter of using your hands to apply pressure. You apply the power, the beauty. When I think that I can't play the way I want to play, I'll hang up my sticks."[31]

While eating a rich Italian meal in a fine New York restaurant, Buddy Rich ended his interview with Balliett by recounting the tale of a college kid who asked Buddy, "Who is the greatest drummer in the world?"[32] Buddy said that he himself was. The kid couldn't believe it, but Rich insisted. He didn't believe in false humility—or perhaps any humility. Ted Williams hadn't tipped his hat when he hit home runs. He was just doing his job, and that's what Buddy said he was doing. He just thought he did it better than anyone else. That may be why there was some controversy about his contribution to the art of jazz drumming. He was a very difficult man to get along with—but beloved for his great talent and ability, especially for his solos, by the best and brightest stars in jazz. Papa Jo Jones, himself never known for his humility, said he didn't know if Rich had learned anything from him, but he had learned from Buddy Rich. Rich lived until April 2, 1987.

"Papa" Jo Jones, born Jonathan Jones in Chicago in 1911, began his career as a tap dancer and toured with carnivals. In the late 1920s, he met bassist Walter Page, who was leading a group called the Blue Devils in Oklahoma City. Jones played with Page for a while, then left to play with a trumpeter's band in Nebraska. After a while, he headed to

Kansas City and met Count Basie there in 1934. When Basie formed his own group, Jones joined, and so did Walter Page. Soon Jones and Page took a brief leave from Basie to play in a well-known regional band in the Midwest. They returned to Kansas City in 1936, joined Basie again, and became part of his celebrated, four-man rhythm section known in the jazz world as the All-American rhythm section, including a guitarist, bassist, Basie, and Jones.

Jones earned his reputation as the most influential swing-era drummer, in part by keeping time on the hi-hat cymbal instead of playing four to the bar only on the bass drum, and by using the bass drum for accents. That's how he revolutionized the drummer's role and priorities; instead of imitating the staccato technique of earlier jazz drummers, Jones made the drum's role more subtle and responsive to solo improvisation. He stressed four even beats in a bar—a technique characteristic of the later swing period. He was never a flashy drummer, a self-serving showman, or an attention-grabbing soloist, as Gene Krupa and bandleader Chick Webb were. But Jones's technique and solos sparkled, hypnotizing other drummers and all listeners.

Papa Jo used his cymbals—the ride and the hi-hats—to such beautiful effect, especially for support and enhancement behind soft-toned tenor saxophonist Lester Young, that their records are considered by some critics to be the best Young ever made. Young in turn was regarded as one of the most influential modern jazz saxophonists.

Some people thought Jo Jones's artistry had its roots in his instincts as a tap dancer. But his innovations with the hi-hat in the mid-1930s were emulated and extended by the drummers of the bebop school beginning in the 1940s. Jo Jones earned his nickname "Papa" for exactly the reason that he was the father of all modern drummers.

He left Basie's band in 1948 and later ran a drum school in Harlem. Lucky was the student who learned directly from the master. Many drummers would recall the effect Papa Jo had on them; they treasured any rare word of praise they ever heard from him. Drummer Grady Tate

Papa Jo Jones

once recalled a time that Jones cuffed him with the sticks to stop him from making a certain mistake. Other drummers had similar memories.

In the early 1980s, Jones had a regular gig on Monday nights in a New York City club, although he was sick. He wasn't playing well anymore. But other drummers showed up in droves, with love and respect in their hearts and sometimes tears in their eyes. Jones died in New York in 1985. If jazz historians and critics had to try to pick the most important drummer for the development of jazz, and the one they never tired of hearing play, Papa Jo Jones would probably win the most votes.

Swing-era drummers themselves would agree on two things: one, that Jones was their master, and two, that if any of them ever got in trouble during a performance, the answer was, as Jones and Buddy Rich and others advised, to play a roll—roll for dear life. Jones, other drummers thought, had all the answers, and you can hear them in the beauty of his playing.

Author's note: There were other early drummers, who didn't achieve fame or invent new techniques, but they made a deep impression on their colleagues and broadened everyone's admiration of the art of jazz drumming. Among the best have been early New Orleans drummer Tony Sbarbaro; Tommy Benford; Bill Beason; Keg Purnell; O'Neil Spencer, who impressed Duke Ellington's first drummer Sonny Greer; Cliff Leeman; Lee Young, the brother of tenor saxophonist Lester Young, who played with Nat King Cole's group and whose brush techniques were much admired; Gus Johnson; Panama Francis, a star in his own groups; Kansas Fields, who can be heard on Sarah Vaughan's recordings made for Mercury in Europe in the 1960s; Denzil Best, who had to give up playing the trumpet because of illness and instead became a fine drummer; Osie Johnson; Tiny Kahn; and Sam Woodyard who played with Duke Ellington after Sonny Greer.

CHAPTER FIVE
THE BEBOP REVOLUTION

No sooner did the swing era get into high gear than an ambitious group of young musicians decided it would be fun and artistically challenging to make jazz more complicated and driving. They called their style of music progressive jazz. By the mid-1940s, journalists called it bebop because the sound of the music, particularly its rhythms and the titles of some of the songs, suggested that name.

Exactly when and where bebop began to develop isn't entirely certain. No one person invented it, but drummer Kenny Clarke was one of its most important innovators.

In 1940, trumpeter Dizzy Gillespie, playing in Cab Calloway's band, passed through Kansas City. As soon as he stepped off the bus, an old friend greeted him and said, "Hey, man. There's a saxophonist you have got to hear. His name is Charlie Parker."

Dizzy checked into a room at the Booker T. Washington Hotel, which was for African-Americans only. Right away, Dizzy's friend brought Charlie "Bird" Parker, a big man with a deep, quiet, baritone voice, into the room and introduced Bird to Dizzy. Bird took out his saxophone and started playing. His phrasing, with its new emphases, fascinated Dizzy. "I can't believe the way he is playing," Dizzy later wrote in his autobiography, *To Be or Not to Bop*. "I've never heard anything like his style before." Dizzy took out his trumpet and began to play, too.

"Bird played the blues like nobody else in the world. As fast as anyone else in the world. Keys didn't make no difference to him. I said, 'Here's the man.' I was completely convinced here was the Jesus of music. We played all day. We forgot to eat."

Dizzy left town with the band the next day. But he would see Bird a great deal over the next couple of years, because they played together in Earl Hines's swing-era band and started to experiment together after hours in Minton's Playhouse and Clark Monroe's Uptown House. The progressives jammed regularly in those places in the early 1940s and developed their new style.

At around the same time that Dizzy and Bird began to elaborate and change the harmonies of the old standard and pop songs, pianist Thelonious Monk and drummer Kenny Clarke were working together in the house trio at Minton's Playhouse. Minton's was regarded as one of the hippest clubs in town. People went there to dance and listen to music on the cutting edge. Monk and Clarke, too, were working on the harmonies and rhythms of jazz, making the music more complex. Monk, an avid student of Duke Ellington's harmonies and the use of dissonance, taught Dizzy a great deal about harmonies. Dizzy worked for hours with Kenny Clarke, too, exploring the way the harmonies and rhythms supported each other.

The seeds of bebop didn't bloom suddenly in the midst of the New York jazz scene. In the previous decade, bebop was prepared for by tenor saxophonist Lester Young's airy, light tone and relaxed swing.

Guitarist Charlie Christian played smooth, long phrases on his guitar, in a manner advanced beyond the strummed-rhythm guitar style that characterized early jazz. Jimmy Blanton, a bassist with a big sound in the Duke Ellington band, played long, melodic phrases. His music was a far cry from the slap bass style of his early jazz predecessors. And Papa Jo Jones had set the stage for progressive drummers by playing the rhythm in a light, legato, dancing style on the hi-hat and using the bass drum more for support and accents.

The big change for the new style took place in the rhythm. The four-beat bar was subdivided into an eighth-note measure. The eight pulses per measure meant there would be a great deal more activity and intensity in the music.

Kenny Clarke was the first drummer to leave behind the clear four-beat swing rhythm. He maintained a continuous pulse on the ride cymbal at the top of his drum set. Instead of keeping time with the bass drum, the snare drum, and the hi-hat, he used them to play cross-rhythms and accents (bombs), which could fall anywhere in a measure of music. (However, Clarke and the beboppers never abandoned the bass drum for playing four beats to the bar; they feathered it—struck it lightly—still using the foot pedal.)

Right away, a younger drummer, Max Roach, listening at Minton's Playhouse, understood and picked up the polyrhythmic style from Kenny Clarke and embellished it further. Max's mature drumming style would be both intense and intimate; he could build a long, fiery, and fascinating drum solo; he could accompany the melody line with brilliance and smoothness. Another youngster, Art Blakey, would soon learn the bebop style from Dizzy, a great teacher of young musicians. Art, too, would go on to have an illustrious career, as Max Roach did.

Bebop melodies became very complex. The chords of songs were altered, and improvisations were played on the new chords. Bebop characteristically employed the higher intervals of the scale, beyond the eight notes of the octave, and used unusual intervals like the flatted fifth tone

Kenny Clarke

of the scales. Flatted fifths became an emblem of bebop. New chords were invented to accompany the melodic innovations. In such ways, the beboppers wrote completely new songs based on the chords of the old songs. The chords of the old Gershwin standard, "I Got Rhythm," for example, gave rise to hundreds of new songs. "How High the Moon," "Indiana," and "Cherokee," popular standards, also provided the chord structures for countless new songs. Thelonious Monk wrote entirely fresh compositions based on his experiments with chords; his tunes were especially beautiful. All the beboppers began writing their own songs.

For a while, most audiences and music critics resisted bebop's odd sounds and said they consisted of wrong notes. Actually, to play bebop, musicians needed a well-defined rhythmic sense, a knowledge of harmony, and virtuosic abilities on their instruments.

Kenny Clarke taught himself most of the techniques he knew, but he had studied drums to a degree. "I went to a drum school during the two or three years I was working in cabarets," he told drummer Art Taylor about the period in his life before he arrived in New York. "I also had a private teacher and started developing myself. At that time there weren't any real drum teachers, just snare-drum, tambour or side-drum teachers. They didn't know much about the bass drum or cymbals in those days, and so it was a sort of self-development project." He also had some knowledge of harmonies from studying the piano.[1]

Clarke, the oldest of the bebop revolutionaries, was born on January 9, 1914, in Pittsburgh, Pennsylvania. By the mid-1950s, he had made his home permanently in France. Because he played in the United States so rarely after that, he lost out on the exposure that would have earned him greater recognition for his accomplishments in his native country. But in France he became a star.

He began in music by taking piano lessons, influenced by his mother, a pianist. But she died when Kenny was seven. He didn't bother with music again until he started playing a snare drum in a school marching band when he was twelve. At fifteen, he stopped playing music again.

Then, in high school, kids could take instruments home with them for practice, so Kenny began rehearsing with his friends in small groups.

When he was eighteen, he started playing in bands in his hometown, then went on the road with a band, and ended up performing in a Cincinnati supper-club show for a couple of years. He also played in a St. Louis club, which he felt prepared him for a career in music. He could read music and play a show. By the end of the 1930s, he arrived in New York.

Playing in Teddy Hill's band, he met Dizzy Gillespie. Soon Hill became manager of Minton's Playhouse and hired Kenny for the house band. Clarke was the primary drummer in the experimentations of the beboppers and helped develop many of the improvisational techniques for the phrasing and harmonies of the progressive style. He acquired his nickname, "Klook" (sometimes "Klook-mop"), in the early 1940s, probably because of the offbeat accents he placed in the music.

He served in the army during World War II, stationed in the segregated South during 1943, then in Europe for two years until 1945. He later reflected that the wonderful people he met in Europe convinced him to move there. He also became a Muslim, changing his name to Liaquat Ali Salaam. He would always feel a deep distrust of the social system in the United States because of the racial situation.

In Europe, he began playing trombone, because it was easier to carry around than drums. But he never took anything except the drums seriously. Before going into the army, he had married Carmen McRae, a young singer and pianist, but their marriage didn't outlast his stint in the service. By the time he came home in 1946, he hadn't played drums for more than a year and a half. "I had been planning to quit playing music because I was kind of disgusted with everything at that time," he told fellow drummer Arthur Taylor. "I guess a lot of soldiers felt that way on returning home to start a new life. Dizzy talked me into playing again, and so I did."[2]

During the next few years, he traveled back and forth between the United States and Europe; he played for his then ex-wife Carmen McRae's first recordings in the 1950s, when she was becoming a star, and he played with Dizzy Gillespie for important early bebop recordings. In 1951, Clarke joined the bebop vibist Milt Jackson's quartet, which evolved a few years later into the Modern Jazz Quartet (MJQ), one of the most important and long-lived groups in jazz history. But Kenny chafed at restrictions imposed upon him by John Lewis, the MJQ's pianist, and in 1955 Kenny left the group.

By 1956, he was living in Paris. There he became a well-known, highly respected figure in the music world. He played with famous bebop pianist Bud Powell and founded the Clarke-Boland Octet with a French musician named Francy Boland. It grew into the Clarke-Boland Big Band, a highly respected band employing both European and American jazz musicians.

Kenny Clarke co-composed several important bebop songs of the 1940s, including "Salt Peanuts," done with Dizzy Gillespie, and "Epistrophy," which evolved with Thelonious Monk and Clarke. "Epistrophy" became Monk's theme song. Clarke may also have helped to compose the "52nd Street Theme" with Monk, though Monk alone received the composer's credit for that song. Everybody played it in the 52nd Street clubs.

Clarke was a very sensitive, creative, and adventurous drummer, whose work served as a touchstone for all drummers involved in the bebop revolution and styles that evolved from it.

Dizzy Gillespie won the New Star award from *Esquire* magazine's jazz poll in 1944, and bassist Oscar Pettiford won the magazine's Gold Star. Together they were asked to lead a group for the Onyx Club on 52nd Street. Pettiford was aided by modern amplification equipment, which made it easier than ever for audiences to hear the bass. Dizzy asked young drummer *Max Roach* to play with the group, since Kenny Clarke was in the army. This gig was bebop's debut on Swing Street—a high-profile position for the new music.

Over the years, Max Roach became far better known to the American public than Kenny Clarke. Critics would even say that Max was a

Max Roach

more creative and imaginative drummer with a lighter touch than Kenny Clarke. And Max took part in a great many milestones of jazz over the next five decades, recording in important groups beginning in the 1940s. He was always the first choice, in Clarke's absence, for Dizzy's and Bird's groups.

In the 1950s, he played in what was called the Greatest Jazz Concert Ever, held at Massey Hall in Toronto, Canada, along with Dizzy, Bird, Bud Powell on piano, and the courageous, very creative bassist Charles Mingus. Mingus, who was trying to get his private record label, Debut, off the ground, had a business partnership with Max Roach. They taped the concert, but Mingus ended up forfeiting the tape to his second wife as part of an alimony settlement. None of the musicians were ever paid a penny for their work on the recording when it was released. Most of them, including Max, were never even paid for the concert, either, because the paychecks bounced.

Max suffered through many of the same difficulties that other African-Americans faced. He would become very politically inclined, writing such pieces as "Freedom Now." In conversations and interviews, he would express exceptionally bitter criticism of whites. Yet he would eventually enjoy greater honors and more respect and financial rewards than almost any other jazz musician. Not only did he have the prestige of becoming a professor of music at the University of Massachusetts at Amherst, but he also received a MacArthur Award (the so-called "genius" award) for American artists. His rich, full career became the envy and the pride of many of his colleagues.

He was born on January 10, 1924, in New Land, North Carolina, in a particularly pretty area, on the edge of a body of water called Dismal Swamp. Max later told an interviewer it was properly named. His family farmed and hunted there, but, when Max was still a child, they moved to the African-American neighborhood of Bedford-Stuyvesant in Brooklyn, New York, hoping for a better life. When his parents went out to work, they put Max and their other children in a storefront Baptist church. It served as an unofficial day-care center tended by neighborhood women. One of them was his aunt, a church organist.

She began teaching Max to play piano. A few years later, when he joined a Boy Scout troop affiliated with the church, he started playing drums. Occasionally he got a chance to see and hear drum sets played at rent parties. Then his father gave him the great encouragement of buying him a drum set with "two Chinese tom-toms, one cymbal, a high-hat (*sic*), a snare drum and a bass drum" to celebrate Max's graduation from Public School 54.[3]

He didn't know what he was doing, banging away on the drums, but he loved them. Perhaps he had inherited talent from the numerous church musicians and blues players in his family. He also paid attention to the big bands playing jazz that he heard on the radio.

He would come to detest the word "jazz," outspokenly focusing on its nearly century old roots as a description for sexual activity. He wouldn't like the word "bebop" either. He thought these words were part of white America's insulting treatment of African-Americans. Friend and colleague Art Blakey, who grew up as a drummer in the bebop era, would believe that nobody remembered the roots of the word jazz, and Blakey was well pleased with the word and the aura it elicited in the long run. Blakey, who also became a Muslim and changed his name to Buhaina, didn't criticize Max for his opinion. But the ways the men viewed these words typified their different attitudes and approaches to society in general—and even to their drumming styles—Max's light, refined, and intense, and Blakey's hard-hitting and earthy. And Max would always say that jazz drumming was a pure African art. Blakey would say it was an African-American and an American invention, having little to do with Africa. (Experts have often theorized that Native American drumming traditions had a great influence on African-American jazz.)

Max was typical of all the drummers in the way he learned to appreciate and play jazz. "Baby Dodds and some of those other early percussionists, they would play the song. They weren't trying to show how fast and loud they could play. And there were a lot of polyrhythms in New Orleans drumming," Max told writer Charles Fox.[4] Max appreciated O'Neil Spencer's use of brushes with the John Kirby sextet, which had a run of several years as a very popular group in New York. And Max thought Gene Krupa's use of brushes was extraordinary, too. He loved Sonny Greer's elaborate drum set. "He brought my attention to the rudimental (*sic*) military style. He was the technical man," said Max. He and his friends especially loved to listen to Count Basie's band on the radio. They loved Chick Webb ("the first major drum soloist I know of," Max said about Chick) and Sid Catlett ("he had fast hands but what affected me was how he played the character of a piece, structuring a solo in almost a classical manner"). Most of all Max loved Jo Jones.

"Jo Jones was the first drummer that I heard who played broken rhythm. He'd break the rhythm behind Prez—that was Lester Young, Basie's tenor man. You'd hear the bass drum breaking up the time. That was long before we started experimenting with all those different polymeters and superimposition of time, things like that," he told Fox.

Attending Boys High, still drumming with other teenagers, Max began working in little shows in Coney Island, "behind fire-eaters and in sideshows," wrote Fox.[5] Max worked round the clock for some gigs, beginning early in the morning and finishing in the wee hours the next day. And he went to hear wonderful bands at the Apollo Theater and Chick Webb's house band at the Savoy Ballroom.

Since he was too young to go into the army and he could read music, Max began to get good jobs to replace the professional drummers who were drafted for World War II. Eventually he went to the Manhattan School of Music with the intention of majoring in drumming. But a teacher discouraged him, Max said, insisting that he use a classical technique that would have hampered him from fitting in with groups on 52nd Street. He switched to a composition major.

And he either sat in at both Minton's and Clarke Monroe's Uptown House, or he may have actually had a job as house drummer at Monroe's. He definitely caught the ears of influential musicians. He recorded with Coleman Hawkins's quintet in December 1943, when he was nineteen, and then he went into a studio the next year with Hawkins and Dizzy, tenor saxophonist Don Byas, pianist Clyde Hart and Oscar Pettiford—all leading musicians of the era.

That year, Roach became the most important drummer in bebop, because he worked with Dizzy's group at the Onyx Club on 52nd Street, then went on tour with Benny Carter's orchestra. That was Roach's first important big band job, except for a few days he spent as a substitute for Sonny Greer at the Paramount Theater. Roach was panicked, because he didn't see any drum music there with Ellington's band. Ellington smiled and told him to keep one eye on him and the other eye on the act.

Max had already become friends with Charlie "Bird" Parker and the young trumpeter Miles Davis. They visited Max's house in Brooklyn. And he played in a group co-led by Parker and Dizzy Gillespie at the Three Deuces on 52nd Street in 1945. Then he worked in Parker's quintet, which included Miles. Bird astounded Max by playing four different rhythms on four different parts of the drum set at once. Max couldn't do exactly what Bird had just done without practicing.

Max went on a tour of the South with Dizzy's first big band, which, naturally, played bebop. Those were rough days for the band. Segregation made it tremendously difficult for musicians to find places to eat and sleep. And people down South wanted to hear the blues and dance. Dizzy's band failed. Back in New York, Max worked with Bird again in 1947. Bird set such fast tempos that Max had to adjust the way he played. But the experience helped him to mature.

He worked with his own group and as a member of the package show Jazz at the Philharmonic, and he drummed briefly in the movie

Carmen Jones. By the mid-1950s, he was ready to start his own band with trumpeter Clifford Brown, who had a strong, brilliant, clear sound. Max would later remember how they roomed together for a while and raced each other to the piano in the mornings to work on compositions.

Their group made some classic recordings and, though it wasn't making a great deal of money, played in respected clubs. On the way to one of their gigs in Chicago, Brown and the group's piano player, Richie Powell, and his wife, the driver of the car, were killed in an accident. Roach was so devastated that he began to drink heavily. He later said that he went to a hospital to be cured of a drinking problem. It may have been around this time, too, that he went back to his relatives in North Carolina, taking himself out of his New York, jazz-world environment, to kick a heroin habit. Years later, he spoke of his cure.

By the end of the 1950s, Max, with other musicians, organized the Alternative Festival to George Wein's official Newport Jazz Festival, claiming that Wein ignored the musicians in the Alternative Festival. In 1961, turning blatantly political, Max began public activism for his views. But it was his music that survived the period—for example, his "Freedom Now," originally intended to celebrate the 100th year of the Emancipation Proclamation of January 1863. Max later explained that it was never finished because he and Oscar Brown, Jr., who worked with him closely on the project, couldn't agree on where they were going with it. Max also wrote music memorializing children who had been killed by a racist's bomb in Birmingham, Alabama, and paying tribute to Marcus Garvey—a piece called "Garvey's Ghost."

In clubs in the 1960s, Max was prone to give speeches. The owner of the Village Vanguard, Max Gordon, asked him to stick to playing the drums. But Roach continued speaking his mind as well as writing his politically assertive music.

In 1970, he organized his all-percussion group called M'Boom Re: Percussion, to showcase jazz and improvisation. At first, people thought Max was crazy, with "eight guys on drum sets!" as he was told by CBS. But he explained that he was including all the mallet instruments — xylophone and marimba as well as timpani and all the rest. He employed eight men who played perhaps 100 percussion instruments between them, and he would play at times with a percussion ensemble to fascinated audiences for the rest of the century.

In 1971, he started his career as an educator at the University of Massachusetts. He also toured in Europe with his small, mainstream jazz group. It was more difficult for acoustic mainstream jazz to find audiences in rock and fusion-happy America by that time. Fusion groups blended acoustic and electric instruments. Though Max would say that he felt electric instruments were excellent because they were created by God, he didn't play with them.[6] So his college teaching career started at the right moment for him.

He would eventually organize a string quartet including his very gifted, viola-playing daughter, Maxine. It was an exceptionally innovative group that played music from the African-American culture — blues, gospel, jazz, and original music by members of the group — in a chamber group setting. Maxine transposed her father's famous drum solo from the suite *Billy the Kid*, so that each member of the quartet, The Uptown String Quartet, played a separate part, each based on what Max's hands and feet had played. The oddly whirling piece was nominated for a Grammy. Although the chamber music setting didn't become commercially successful, the group occasionally recorded and played in clubs and concerts with Max's own jazz group. A fascinating idea to begin with, the group won praises from critics.

Late in his life, Max frequently played drum solos and appeared in concerts in prestigious halls in collaboration with dancers and poets as well as musicians. Tall, lean, erect, and distinguished-looking into his seventies, he played the drums with elegance and class. With Dizzy Gillespie in Paris in 1989, he collaborated on an album *Max Plus Dizzy*, on A&M Records, which included a long conversation between the men about the old days—not necessarily the "good old days," since they had so many unhappy memories about bebop's struggle for recognition and about racial prejudice. But they delivered their opinions and memories with wit and pungency. The men had survived to enjoy great success—and to have the last laugh.

All jazz drummers realized the debt they owed Max Roach for his persistence, high standards for drumming, virtuosity, and creativity, and for his forward-thinking approach to jazz and its future.

THE JAZZ DRUMMING TREE

Here is an overview of jazz drumming styles, from the early, swing-era drummers to the beboppers to the modernists. Many times the categories overlap, since quite a few drummers spanned nearly all the eras. No matter when they began playing, those versatile drummers were able to adapt themselves and fit in with nearly any style that developed.

The earliest jazz drummers using full drum sets for ragtime combined simple, march-like figures with syncopation and improvisation, including the rudiments—the generally accepted techniques, or patterns—played on drums. The earliest drummers rarely used cymbals, except for punctuation or surprise.

The rudiments—set patterns of drum beats—were used in nearly every jazz style throughout the century. Every drummer must learn the rudiments from teachers, role models or books. First of all, players must learn how to hold the drumsticks and develop a grip. The rudiments include, perhaps first and foremost, the roll. By playing a roll, a drummer can hold a note, for a *roll* is a series of uninterrupted beats, without rhythmic stresses, played at a speed to give the effect of a flowing line. There are many variations on the basic roll. The press roll favored by Baby Dodds and other early jazz drummers produced a slightly buzzing sound accomplished by rapidly repeating single beats.

There are many other rudiments that every drummer must master—grace notes such as the *flam*, played with the proper speed and finger control, and the basic *paradiddle*, effected by the right and left hands working together, and the *ratamacue*, which is a triplet preceded by a grace note and followed by a single stroke. There are countless combinations of such rudiments as these, and lesson books and schools provide exercises for playing all parts of drum sets.

Drummers raised in the New Orleans style during the first two decades of the twentieth century invented varied patterns to accompany the front-line musicians, who were primarily horn players—trumpeters, trombonists and, clarinetists.[1] The most famous of these New Orleans drummers were *Baby Dodds* and *Zutty Singleton.* Drummers by the 1920s were part of a rhythm section; it often consisted of piano, tuba or banjo, drums, and guitar in the 1920s, and definitely, by the 1930s, of a piano, double-string bass, drums, and guitar.

In the 1920s, in the North, particularly in Chicago, players often studied music formally, and they had a chance to hear the music of many types of groups who passed through town and to incorporate their influences. It was important for the Chicago drummers to learn from the New Orleans pioneers. And Chicago drummers used the cymbal for rhythmic accompaniment, the bass drum playing four beats to the bar in tandem with other instruments, and wire brushes for fills—improvised embellishments—for the front-line musicians.

By the end of the 1920s, some drummers began to concentrate on playing a "hot cymbal" style, as they called it, using the hi-hat cymbal. It was particularly important for the developing art of jazz drumming, because it allowed drummers to break away from emphasizing that rigid four-beat pattern on the bass drum, with solos on the snare drums or occasionally on tom-toms, in favor of a greater show of musicianship combined with attention-getting techniques.

During this period, *Gene Krupa* became the best-known drummer of his generation to the general public. However some of his contemporaries were just as skilled or even more so.

GENE KRUPA

(right) with Tommy Dorsey

Among them were *Davey Tough, Buddy Rich, Cozy Cole, Papa Jo Jones, Sonny Greer, Chick Webb*, and *"Big" Sid Catlett*.

Also from the 1920s into the 1940s, when big bands for dancing became very popular, drummers modified their styles to fit into their groups' arrangements. Drummers still improvised their parts. But bandleaders and arrangers often made suggestions to drummers about what parts of the drum set and which techniques to use. Big band drummers often used the hi-hat for hot cymbal playing; among the players noted for their use of the hi-hat were *Kaiser Marshall*, followed by *Walter Johnson*, both in Fletcher Henderson's band, highly regarded for its arrangements. Johnson's playing on the cymbals became legato—he played long lines, or four beats to the bar, on the cymbals. By so doing, he made the choked cymbal technique—the sparing use of the cymbal common among earlier drummers—sound old-fashioned.

The most spectacular drummer in the big bands was *Chick Webb*, leader of his own band, who elevated the drummer's position with his showmanship and techniques for accompaniment and soloing. He could accurately be called the first true soloist on drums.

By the late 1930s, drummers were using the ride cymbal to accompany soloists. *Davey Tough* in Tommy Dorsey's popular swing-era band and then in many other bands

DAVEY TOUGH

and Papa Jo Jones in Count Basie's band became standard setters for this innovative style of playing. Jones's fame for his work on the cymbals overrode everyone else's, and his influence on the bebop drummers of the 1940s became legendary. He kept time on the hi-hat and feathered the bass drum—played it with a light touch—for support for 4/4 time.

By this time, the rhythm in the music had changed noticeably. Count Basie was quoted in the liner notes of an out-of-print Decca album as saying, "I don't dig that two-beat jive the New Orleans cats play, 'cause my boys and I got to have four heavy beats to the bar and no cheating." And he was quoted making a similar comment by Len Lyons for his book about the best jazz albums.[2] Actually New Orleans musicians played four to the bar, too, but their style was staccato, and in swing music the rhythm became smoother. Instead of emphasizing syncopation, an irregularity in the beat, swing musicians played with a greater flow. They didn't accentuate each stroke of the beat so clearly as the New Orleans musicians did.

Critic Robert Palmer, who wrote liner notes for an anthology of drum styles called *The Drums* on the Impulse label, explained that drummer *Sid Catlett*, who played with a small group led by New Orleans trumpeter Louis Armstrong, "was seen and heard, while *Jo Jones* was often simply felt." Palmer emphasized the new smoothness of the drum lines. No matter what the differences were between the bands—and each had its distinctive sound—all drummers emphasized sophistication and urbanity. Gone was the suggestion of country music in the New Orleans style.

In the 1940s, the bebop drummers, inspired by Jo Jones's cymbal work on the hi-hat first and foremost, used the ride cymbal as their primary instrument for accompaniment. They consistently employed the hi-hat for the second and fourth beats of the bar. And they punctuated their work with "bombs"—accents—on the bass drum instead of playing loudly on the bass as a primary timekeeping technique. They feathered the bass drum instead, playing it as a virtual undercurrent.

Bebop drummers, accompanying front line instrumentalists, began playing four separate, though coordinated, rhythms with both hands and feet. The best known, most influential drummers who helped establish the bebop style were *Kenny Clarke* and the younger *Max Roach*.

Clarke first played the new, modern style at a club called Minton's in Harlem, where young, up-and-coming musicians such as trumpeter Dizzy Gillespie, alto saxophonist Charlie Parker, and pianist Thelonious Monk worked on making harmonies more complex. They also changed the phrasing of songs and wrote new ones based on the chords of old ones. Drummers intensified the new music and quickened the pace.

All through the century, the rhythm of jazz was increasingly stepped up—with whole notes subdivided into halves or 2/4 time, or two beats per measure for ragtime, then divided again with syncopated quarter notes, 4/4 time, in New Orleans-style music, and then more fully subdivided into quarter notes, in 4/4 time, in the swing era, and then subdivided further into eighth notes—eight beats to the measure—for bebop's frenetic modern pace.

For the faster tempos of the bebop style, Kenny Clarke played a continuous pulse on the ride cymbal. He feathered the bass drum and used it, the snare drum, and hi-hat cymbal to play cross rhythms and to accent the music with "bombs," which could be played anywhere in a measure of music. *Max Roach*, about ten years younger than Clarke, and then an even younger drummer, *Art Blakey*, played music directly taken from Clarke's style. As part of the house trio at Minton's in 1940 and 1941, Clarke worked out the drummer's new role with Thelonious Monk on a nightly basis. Roach would take the ideas for drumming even further.

Maintaining his importance in the 1940s was Big Sid Catlett, actually a swing-era drummer whose virtuosity was so great that he could incorporate the bebop style and play with Bird. And Sid was especially generous about advising younger players how to improve their craft. Everyone paid attention to his technique and tastefulness. And he was constantly in demand for jobs. *Ed Thigpen* was another popular drummer of the bebop style. And *Stan Levey*, a young white Philadelphian, found work with important bebop groups, especially those of his mentor Dizzy Gillespie, who thought Levey had a great deal of talent and ability.

Doffing their hats and paying strict attention to the work of the beboppers were youngsters on all the instruments who wanted to write their own innovations into the history books. The styles of music they played were divided into three types: the cool school, hard bop, and Third Stream.

The cool school musicians played in a style developed by trumpeter Miles Davis with pianist and arranger Gil Evans. Particularly influenced by Duke Ellington's music with its unusual harmonies, Evans had been the arranger for the smooth, beautiful, mood-evoking sound of the big band, with its mastery of dynamics, led by Claude Thornhill. And Gil Evans had also fallen in love with the haunting sound of Miles Davis's trumpet in the early bebop groups. Those groups played very fast music in the 1940s. But Evans understood that Miles as a young man was suited to playing a slower paced music in the middle register of the trumpet at that time. And Miles wanted to do away with the glut of chords that had taken over the improvising and composing styles of the beboppers.

Miles substituted modes—a series of notes with a tonal center—instead of chords for the new cool school music he invented with Evans in the late 1940s. (In 1949, Kenny Clarke recorded a tune called "Boplicity," included on Miles Davis's album *Birth of the Cool*, done with Gil Evans as arranger.)

Involved in the cool school and part of the Davis-Evans nonet—a nine-piece group—that played on *Birth of the Cool* was baritone saxophonist Gerry Mulligan. In the early 1950s, he moved to Los Angeles, California, where he formed a pianoless quartet including drummer **Chico Hamilton**. The men played laid-back, dreamy-sounding music; it seemed to reflect the California landscape that served as home base for the quartet. Gil Evans himself had grown up in California. Critics often thought that his early life there, which revolved around a beach culture, had influenced his conception of the haunting, mellow way jazz should sound.

MAX ROACH

Mel Lewis, though he referred to himself as a bebopper,[3] was sometimes categorized as a cool school drummer. He traveled on the road with the modern-sounding big band of Stan Kenton, an adventurer in harmonies. After that job, Mel played in New York recording studios and then collaborated with famed trumpeter and composer Thad Jones. They formed a modern big band based in the Village Vanguard, a leading New York jazz club. Lewis's accompaniment for Thad's compositions was especially tasteful. **Shelly Manne**, too, who became well known for playing in small groups, was categorized as a cool school drummer. He eventually opened his own jazz club in Los Angeles and called it Shelly's Manne-hole.

Establishing his own category in this period, pianist Ahmad Jamal formed a trio with Israel Crosby on bass and New Orleans-born **Vernel Fournier** on drums. The trio, with its innovative idea for allowing space for all the musicians to solo, became world famous with its recordings in the mid-1950s. Its interpretation of "Poinciana," one of the best-known songs in its repertoire, became a classic jazz recording.

ELVIN JONES

Fournier's taste and subtlety graced many groups for the rest of the century.

Another offshoot of the beboppers, the hard boppers acquired their name for almost as mysterious a reason as their precursors became known as beboppers. The foremost hard-bop drummer, **Art Blakey**, said the word "bebop" came from Dizzy Gillespie, who used to entitle his songs by such scat-type words as "Oo Bop Sh Bam," and "Ool Ya Koo." Journalists coined the word *bebop* to emulate the sound of the song titles.

Beboppers often played the blues; Charlie Parker was a great blues player and even a composer in the blues form. But Dizzy Gillespie and others involved in bebop were not particularly known for their blues playing. They concentrated on modernizing the harmonies, phrasing, and tempos of songs.

Hard boppers, taking part of their inspiration from bebop, began to concentrate on playing the blues and church-music roots of jazz forcefully and soulfully. Art Blakey, who went to Dizzy Gillespie's "school"—that is, who took his coaching from Dizzy—went on to become a very influential hard-bop drummer. He formed his own hard-driving group, the Jazz Messengers, and gave scores of musicians on all instruments a chance to play, write, and showcase their own music. The words "hard bop" may have come from the forceful way Blakey beat his drums.

Pianist Horace Silver became a world-famous hard bopper, leading his quintet in such funky, soulful, melodically beautiful and original songs as "Song for My Father" and "Senor Blues," and the lesser-known "Nica's Dream," on which Detroit-born drummer **Roy Brooks** played in the earthy style of his leader.

Art Blakey and drummer *Elvin Jones* (Thad Jones's brother) had some roots, or inspiration, in common. Blakey played for classic recordings in the 1940s and 1950s with pianist Thelonious Monk. Elvin Jones went to play, beginning in 1959, for innovative tenor saxophonist John Coltrane, who had been a starring horn player in a Thelonious Monk quartet in the 1950s. Monk had exerted a great influence on Coltrane's intense style and understanding of harmonies. If there is a group that could epitomize the absolute opposite of the mellow cool school, it is Coltrane's group, in which Elvin, learning from his leader, took long, fiery, loose, and free solos.

Yet another drummer associated with the hard boppers is *Roy Haynes*. Along the road of his long, bright career, he played with Monk in the 1950s and then went on to lead his own groups. But Haynes's roots in professional jazz went back to the swing era, to Luis Russell's band playing New Orleans style music.

Another heir of the bebop style was Third Stream Music. It was a term coined to describe jazz groups that began to emphasize a meeting point between European classical music and jazz. Best known of the Third Stream groups was the Modern Jazz Quartet, whose drummer, *Connie Kay*, collaborated well for the standards set by the group's swinging vibes player, bebopper Milt Jackson, and pianist John Lewis, who was immersed in the European classical tradition.

Other diverse drummers who could be assigned places in the post bebop, hard bop, cool jazz, and Third Stream styles—or who could play in any of those styles with ease because of their training and modern spirit—were bebop-oriented *Philly Joe Jones*, and his friend and colleague *Shadow Wilson*.

Then along came *Tony Williams*, one the most electrifying drummers ever to play in a Miles Davis group. *Louis Hayes* was another drummer with his roots in the styles of the late bebop era. After Tony Williams, *Jack DeJohnnette* played in groups led by Miles Davis. DeJohnnette later won polls consistently as the best

TONY WILLIAMS

jazz drummer in the world. He and Tony Williams and Elvin Jones were the three most famous drummers beginning their careers in the post-bop era.

Paul Motian became associated with pianist Bill Evans and his delicate style in the 1960s, and Motian was construed as a cool jazz player—though he would go on to use electronics when he led his own groups and played, as so many modern drummers would do, under the influence of electronic fusion (jazz-rock) music.

Motian and many other drummers, unlike jazz musicians on other instruments, welcomed the fusion style that became so popular in the 1960s and 1970s. For one thing, fusion emphasized fast, loud, and sometimes funky music and gave drummers more chances to showcase themselves.

In the late 1950s, *Billy Higgins* played in a shocking, free jazz group, whose music sounded cacophonous, without a set time for Higgins to keep. Alto saxophonist Ornette Coleman led that group. Higgins would become one of the most imaginative and sought-after drummers for modern mainstream groups, always playing highly complex, very modern music.

First, Ornette's group made a stir at the Five Spot Cafe in New York and shook up the critics with the "new thing," as it was called. For a little while, the ideas of the free jazz players made a stir. Everyone in Ornette's group played in an ensemble, but everyone played his own part with seemingly little respect for or attention to what the other players were doing. The melodic, harmonic, and rhythmic content of the group's music sounded like a free-for-all to some audiences. It was collectively played, spontaneous improvisation. It would take a long time for the public to accept the dissonances and atonality of free jazz. Miles Davis, for one, thought the free jazz players were crazy. Art Blakey didn't like free jazz either.

Blakey said, "Beethoven and Bach . . . really knew what they were doing. This was their field. The black musician has nothing to do with that. His thing is to swing. . . . Swinging is our field, and we should stay in it. . . . Why should we give up our thing when we've got the greatest thing in the world? We're going out there messing with something else which has no beat, which just goes yang, yang, yang . . . I can put some records on by Beethoven and Bach that would turn you completely around. They're the masters of that. But it's not for us. Our thing is to swing, and it's nothing to be ashamed of. It's something to be proud of."[4]

The free jazz drummers became known for their rhythmic feeling, colors, and accents, which had nothing to do with swinging or timekeeping in the traditional sense of mainstream jazz.

In contrast to the great popularity of rock and fusion groups in the 1960s and 1970s, free jazz players went into commercial eclipse. Their records didn't sell well at all. The musicians played primarily for each other for little or no pay.

Nevertheless, their ideas did influence the spirit and the sound of jazz in general. By the 1980s, when acoustic, traditional jazz became popular with the public again, the jazz drummers—though obviously influenced by the mainstream jazz and fusion players—maintained a curiosity about aspects of free jazz. And all the drummers constantly sought ways to expand the scope of their drum sets and the sound of their playing.

Among the scores of fine young drummers who emerged in the modern era, showing the influences of their predecessors and respectful of the tradition of swing, have been *Kenny Washington, Marvin "Smitty" Smith, Louis Nash, Danny Gottlieb, Cindy Blackman*, and *Terri Lyne Carrington*. And *Dennis Mackrell*, who was born long after the end of the big band era, could take over the drum seat in the surviving big bands and empower those groups with drive and excitement as well as anybody in history had ever done. Known for his work with acoustic and fusion, rock and rhythm and blues players is the versatile and gifted *Steve Gadd*.

So mainstream jazz drummers, fusion jazz drummers, and modern heirs of the free jazz players continue to work their spells.

CHAPTER SIX

LATIN RHYTHMS IN THE BEBOP ERA AND BEYOND

During the 1940s, Dizzy Gillespie masterminded the presentation of the bebop style, publicizing it and bringing it to audiences by a combination of his musicianship and showmanship. One of his most important accomplishments, after the development of harmonies, was to introduce authentic Latin drumming into bebop. Latin musicians would always be grateful to Dizzy for his recognition of them. As late as the end of the twentieth century, they still weren't fully integrated into mainstream jazz in the United States. But there were notable Latin drummers who made an impression on the mainstream because of Dizzy's efforts in the 1940s. The first of these Latin drummers was *Chano Pozo*.

Dizzy was particularly fascinated by the polyrhythmic, Afro-Cuban music that had been developed by the drummers—the conga, timbales, and quinto players—on the island of Cuba. There, musicians had kept alive the drumming traditions of Africa. The black people of Cuba had never been forbidden to play drums.

In 1947, Dizzy told old friend Mario Bauza, a Cuban musician, that he wanted a conga player for his big band. Bauza knew just the man for Dizzy. A conga player named Chano Pozo had just arrived from Cuba. He couldn't speak a word of English, but he was one of the most exciting players Bauza had ever heard. Chano and Dizzy communicated through the language of the drums.

Dizzy would not be able to remember when he first heard and loved the Afro-Cuban rhythms. But he decided to find ways to blend them with the swing of jazz. First he and Chano wrote and played a song they called "Manteca," which means "lard." Dizzy and Chano developed "Manteca" with the help of Dizzy's musical director, Walter Gil Fuller, who gave the song a structure. He arranged and orchestrated it for Dizzy's band. Then Dizzy, Chano, and a modern musician named George Russell wrote "Cubano Be, Cubano Bop." These exciting songs with an exotic flavor were among Dizzy's best-selling recordings.

Chano Pozo lacked discipline. His music needed the development and structure that Walter Gil Fuller could give it. Chano's life was strange and disorganized, too. Dizzy knew him as a "roughneck," even a "hoodlum," who traveled with a long knife, Dizzy said in his autobiography, *To Be or Not to Bop*. Chano was also a great musician who was, in Dizzy's words, "stone African"—completely African. That is, he was a master at playing the African spiritual rhythms that had survived in Cuba.

There were rumors about why Chano left Cuba. One tale said that he had gone to collect royalties from a man there. Instead of paying Chano, the man shot him. Chano went to New York with a bullet lodged dangerously close to his spine. Sometimes it hurt him when he played. Another rumor was that he had taken money dishonestly from his spiritual group in Cuba. But Chano's murky background didn't cloud his music.

His exciting showmanship helped Dizzy spread the message of bebop. The band went into Carnegie Hall for its first concert there on September

29, 1947, not only with Chano but with Charlie Parker. Critics praised the concert, Dizzy, and bebop. Dizzy repeated his success with his band at Carnegie Hall in 1948 and set off for a tour of Europe. He took Chano Pozo, Kenny Clarke, and many other fine players. In France, a concert at the Salle Pleyel was recorded in a primitive way on February 28, 1948, with Chano Pozo as one of the great stars of the show.

Back in the United States, traveling with Dizzy's band down South, Chano Pozo's drums were stolen. He went back to New York, where he was shot to death in the Rio Bar on 111th Street and Fifth Avenue. Dizzy first heard a rumor that a drug dealer had shot Chano. Then Dizzy heard another rumor that he came to think might be true. Chano might have been killed for revenge on the first anniversary of the day he left Cuba with money belonging to his spiritual group. For Dizzy and his band, Chano's death was a big loss. Chano and Dizzy had collaborated for about a year.

In years to come, other Latin drummers would take part in mainstream jazz groups and achieve some success in the United States. Their rhythms weren't really new to the country. Long before jazz had its name, the rhythms of the Caribbean entered the United States, brought to New Orleans by slaves from Haiti, the Spanish-owned islands, and South America. Early in the twentieth century, the rhythmic accents spread to other cities, too. Afro-Cuban rumba and tango rhythms showed up in the music of early jazz stars such as Jelly Roll Morton, W. C. Handy and Cab Calloway.

The difference between Cuban music and all other music is in the rhythms. The instruments—the congas, bongos, timbales, the bata drum, and the agogo, which is a double cowbell—are uniquely Cuban. And there's a different feeling about music in each Latin country. Cuban music has more force than the music of other Latin countries. Brazilian music is basically the samba, which has a soft sound. The Dominican Republic has the relatively simple merengue. Argentina has the seductive tango. But Cuban music has many rhythms and is very complex.

Probably the main inspiration for Cuban music was the church. The Afro-Cuban religions, particularly the Yoruba religion, had their roots in the West African Yoruba tribe, just as the blues and jazz came from the gospel music.

The conga drum is probably the best known of the Cuban instruments. Actually, the instrument is called a *tumba*, and the musician is a *tumbadora*. But there's a rhythm called the *conga*, and that's how the name *conguero* came into being for Cuban conga players. Cuba has sixty-one varieties of rhythms, most of which are unknown outside of Cuba. One of them is *son montuno*, the fast and slow part of the evolution of a piece of dance music. In Puerto Rico, and among Latin musicians who have become popular in America, the son montuna is called *salsa*. Son montuna and salsa use the *clave* as the basis of the rhythm. And so do almost all other types of Cuban music or rhythms—*guaracha, rumba, guaguanco, yambu, yoruba, columbia, macuto, mozambique*, which is a dance rhythm primarily for carnival, and *chaonda*, which is more a spectacle than a popular dance. All but one of Cuba's sixty-one rhythms use the clave—the 3-2 clave for son montuno, and the 2-3 clave for guaguanco and rumba. Each music has its own basic rhythms, but the clave can be played with all of them.

Pat your hand on the table three times, then two times more. Now pat your hand twice, then three times. Those rhythms are the clave, and they have influenced most of the music of Spanish-speaking America. The clave is a profound rhythmic feeling. And it's difficult for musicians to maintain it while they fit in with pianists and bassists.

Among the musicians of Latin background who play Cuban music now is **Ray Mantilla**. His father played a Peruvian-style guitar. But Mantilla, who was born in New York in 1934, heard the music of the Cubans all around him as he was growing up in the East Bronx, and he gravitated toward playing the conga. He soon found himself playing with the Latin stars, whom he loved. Then he crossed over to the mainstream jazz scene. By 1957, Mantilla was playing with Herbie Mann, a popular flutist in mainstream jazz. After that, Mantilla kept moving back

Tito Puente

and forth from Latin to mainstream jazz. He leads his own groups, and he was chosen to play with Max Roach's group M'Boom.

Latin rhythms can be a great study, independent from American jazz rhythms. One of the best-known Latin musicians by the end of the twentieth century was bandleader and timbales player ***Tito Puente***.

HARD BOP, COOL JAZZ, AND THIRD STREAM MUSIC

Other drummers who began their careers in the bebop era went on to distinguish themselves as leaders in the offshoot of bebop called hard bop. They included Art Blakey, Roy Haynes, Philly Joe Jones, Shadow Wilson, Art Taylor, and Stan Levey.

Levey played with Dizzy's bebop group that brought the new music to the West Coast in the mid-1940s.

Shadow Wilson played with pianist Thelonious Monk's groups on recordings and at the Five Spot Cafe, where Monk emerged as a power to be reckoned with—a star as a performer and composer beginning in 1957.

Philly Joe Jones, with his exceptional, individualistic style, became a group leader who inspired many drummers. He, too, played with Monk.

Roy Haynes played with a number of important musicians beginning in the swing era, when he was very young, and went on to win acclaim and prestigious awards in Europe and the United States.

Art Taylor played and recorded with many groups, including Monk's, and went to live in Paris when rock began to dominate the music scene commercially in the United States. Not only did he find enough work in Europe, but he fell in love with the very agreeable lifestyle virtually free of racial prejudice in Paris. There he began to compile a book of interviews done with musicians about their lives, opinions, and musical careers. First he published that book, which he called *Notes and Tones*, at his own expense, and he sold copies to friends. Eventually he published the book with a major publisher in the United States, when he returned to live and lead a group in New York. He achieved recognition for his book as well as for his drumming.

HARD BOP

Of all the drum-playing heirs of bebop, *Art Blakey* became the most illustrious, especially as a nurturer of younger musicians on all the instruments. He made his long-lived group, Art Blakey and the Jazz Messengers, world famous.

Blakey was born in Pittsburgh, Pennsylvania, on October 11, 1919. A short, sturdily built youngster, he barely had a chance to attend school and went to work in the steel mills and coal mines at a very early age. "That's one of the things I would like to forget in my life," he told Art Taylor for *Notes and Tones*.[1] Blakey began to play music because he perceived it as a way to get out of the coal mines. "I would leave music at six in the morning and be at the steel mill by eight. I would work all day, then go to the club at eleven in the evening and work." He taught himself to play in the swinging style of drummers he admired: Chick Webb, Sid Catlett, and Ray Bauduc.

Because he went to work so young and married at age fifteen for the first time, he reflected, "I never really had a childhood." As soon as he could, he got out of town to pursue a career in music, beginning with a job with pianist Mary Lou Williams. They went to West 52nd Street in

Art Blakey (in cowboy hat) with his band, including Kevin Eubanks
(with guitar) and Branford Marsalis (far right)

New York in 1942. The next year, he joined Fletcher Henderson's band
and toured in the South, where the musicians were beaten up. Blakey
later said he hadn't understood the white police down South in those
days. He ended up with a steel plate in his head, and he was told that it
would shorten his life. But it didn't; he lived to a relatively old age.

For a while after that he stayed in Boston, where he met young Roy
Haynes. Roy would later joke about the difference in their ages. When he
and Blakey shared the Apollo Theater's stage for a performance in the
1980s, Blakey called Roy "brother," making it seem as if they were the
same age. Originally, Art "used to call me son," Roy told the audience.

The most important boost for Blakey's career was a job in singer Billy Eckstine's band. "I didn't know what to think of the new style of music. . . . Things were moving so fast . . ." Blakey recalled for Dizzy's autobiography. Billy's musical director was Dizzy Gillespie, who noticed that Blakey couldn't play in the bebop style. Dizzy stopped Blakey in the middle of a performance and asked Blakey what he was doing. Blakey actually said, "I don't know." Dizzy said, "Then why do you do it? If we had wanted a shuffle here, we'd hire Cozy Cole. We want you to play your drums the way *you* play them."[2]

Dizzy taught the young drummer to play by calling out the rhythms in scat language. Dizzy's lifelong friend Bob Redcross would recall, "Diz would get up outta his chair and go put his head right in Blakey's bass drum and stand right down in front of him and be going, 'ooo-bop-she-dow-ooo-bop-bop,' hollering out licks for him and accents for him to play."[3] Blakey learned fast and gratefully.

When he left Eckstine's band in 1947, Blakey began recording for the Blue Note label, whose owners admired his work. Soon he began to lead his own big band called the Seventeen Messengers, a rehearsal band, and then the Jazz Messengers, an octet for performances. He felt a mission to bring the message of jazz to people, and he wanted to give young musicians a band to learn in.

In the late 1940s, he traveled in Africa, where he learned about the music and culture, and converted to Islam, taking the name Abdullah ibn Buhaina. For the rest of his life, his close friends called him Bu and Buhaina. And he developed the theory that African-American jazz drumming was a totally American invention and not as indebted to African drumming as most jazz experts believe. He personally felt more influenced by Kenny Clarke, Max Roach, and Dizzy Gillespie.

Back in the United States, Blakey performed with Charlie "Bird" Parker, Miles Davis, Clifford Brown, and the pianist Horace Silver. He and Silver felt a special kinship, committed to the blues roots of jazz. After recording together, they formed a cooperative group called the Jazz Messengers with tenor saxophonist Hank Mobley and trumpeter Kenny Dorham in 1955. Silver left in 1956, and the leadership of the Jazz Messengers fell to Blakey. He kept the group active for the rest of his life, more than forty years. Through its ranks passed some of the most important bassists, pianists, and horn players of modern jazz.

Blakey insisted that every one of them compose their own music and publish it. He told them that those songs could constitute a valuable legacy to their families for generations to come; their children would benefit from the royalties. If anyone didn't compose, he had to leave the band. And when Blakey deemed a player ready, Blakey made him strike out on his own to make space for a new, young musician. Great horn players—from Lee Morgan, Wayne Shorter, Freddie Hubbard, and Woody Shaw to Wynton Marsalis—joined the Messengers and did spectacular work on records and in performances with the band. Among the important pianists have been Keith Jarrett, James Williams, Mulgrew Miller, Donald Brown, and Joanne Brackeen.

Brackeen would tell an amusing story about how she joined the band. She went to Slug's, a Lower East Side club in Manhattan where Blakey was playing. The pianist was floundering, unable to keep up with the music. Joanne went to the bandstand, sat down at the piano, and played very well. Blakey looked up and saw her. "After that we went to Japan," Joanne recalled. Her career was launched; she went on to play with Joe Henderson and Stan Getz, very important saxophonists, then led her own groups. It was typical of Blakey to disregard the background, race, religion, or gender of a musician. All he cared about was whether a person was talented. Short, stocky Blakey called tall, slender Joanne, a white woman, his "daughter."

Blakey toured constantly with his Jazz Messengers, greeted by critical acclaim and adoring fans around the world. In Japan, where he was idolized, one of his albums was called the best of the year in the early 1990s.

In the early 1970s, he made two world tours with a Giants of Jazz group organized by George Wein, including Dizzy Gillespie, vibist Kai Winding, saxophonist Sonny Stitt, Thelonious Monk, and bassist Al McKibbon.

George Wein's Newport Jazz Festivals often included Art Blakey. He was regarded as one of the great drum masters in jazz, in a league with Max Roach, Buddy Rich, and Elvin Jones, a younger drummer who would become famous in the 1960s with saxophonist John Coltrane.

Blakey was an explosive, loud, intensely exciting, aggressive drummer, who created his own ideas and improvisations, with his hard bop feeling, on the foundation of bebop drumming innovations. Ike Quebec, a well-known saxophonist of the swing era, once described Blakey's style: "Other drummers say thump, Blakey says POW!"[4] He was a master of the press roll, with which he launched soloists into their great improvisations. And he had a lavish, brilliant technique on the ride cymbal. He immersed his audiences completely in his music.

Among his great albums done apart from his work with the Jazz Messengers was a trio album with Thelonious Monk on the Atlantic label and a quintet album called *A Night at Birdland* on the Blue Note label.

Roy Haynes emerged as a very important bebop drummer, though he began his career in the swing era, and he was still going strong in the 1990s, winning awards and enjoying the fruits of his labor. Citing all the years that he has been playing professionally, he summed up his outlook: "Pretty damn good."[5]

As early as the 1950s, he showed up in the *Down Beat* magazine polls in the Talent Deserving Wider Recognition category. And he was in the regular critics' polls when he played with Lester Young. A small man who always looked youthful and trim, Haynes won an award as one of the best-dressed men of the year in *Esquire* magazine in 1959 or 1960, along with Miles Davis.

Born on March 13, 1925, Roy was only six years younger than Art Blakey. *The Encyclopedia of Jazz in the Seventies* said Haynes was born in 1926. "Because I lied," Haynes admitted recently. "I wanted to stay young, which I did anyhow. So I've conquered that." He knew that he looked younger than his seventies. "And you don't have to think about getting older. It thinks about it for you," he philosophized.

In the 1990s, he won a variety of honors. On his birthday in 1993 the Danish prime minister presented him with a $30,000 Jazzpar Prize — essentially the Nobel Prize of jazz. "It was one of the biggest things in my career," he said. "Not for the money, but for the honor." In January 1995, he went to California to play in a group with the young pianist Billy Childs and bassist John Clayton for the American Jazz Masters awards ceremonies, at which Haynes received an award.

Some critics called *Homecoming*, on the Evidence label, his best album. This very contemporary 1994 album, with his aggressive drumming style, was made with his group of young modernists. But there have actually been many great albums in his career, among them *Newport '63*, on the Impulse label with John Coltrane, and his recordings in the trio backing Sarah Vaughan for Mercury in the 1950s. For Sarah, Haynes worked light-years away from the deafening, hard sound of rock drums to come, or even from the aggressive sound of one of his great influences, Art Blakey, or the sparse, intense style of pianist Thelonious Monk, in whose groups Haynes played. And he created masterpieces of loose rhythms that supported and enhanced her. Roy even made moments when she introduced the trio to audiences in clubs exciting. She sang the pianist's name, then went on to bassist "Crazy Joe Benjamin," a name followed by a taut drumbeat, then "Roy," more drumbeats, and "Haynes" followed by a flurry of drumming showmanship. The ritual developed into a song called "Shulie-a-bop." As a sideman and a leader, with his spirit, propulsion, and details, Roy has been the inspiration for milestone performances. He himself has been proud of and inspired by his own track record.

Like Max Roach, he is one of the few masters who can play a mesmerizing drum solo. One night at the Apollo Theater in the mid-1980s, he sat down alone on stage with a drum set and played a graceful, soft, exciting solo with such finesse that the audience cheered.

One of four sons of immigrants from Barbados, Roy liked growing up in the poor, but integrated neighborhood of Roxbury, Massachusetts, near Boston. He found a pair of drumsticks in the house. They belonged to his brother, who played drums in school. "I picked them up, and I had the feeling and rhythm. It was a gift from above, I'm sure." His mother told him she believed he would make some money one day—but she didn't let him play jazz records at home or drums in the house at all on Sundays.

He began bringing money home from his little gigs in town. (Eventually he would be proud when his father went to New York to see Roy play with Charlie "Bird" Parker in November 1949 to open the world-famous club Birdland. His father also came to hear Roy play with Thelonious Monk in the days when Monk with his quartet became a star at the little Greenwich Village club called the Five Spot in 1957. Monk and his quartet made that club famous.)

Roy despised school, and when the principal suspended him for drumming on the desk, Roy quit altogether and devoted himself to playing with groups in town in the early 1940s. When New York-based groups hired a local drummer, it was often Roy. Word of his ability spread in the jazz world. In 1945, bandleader Luis Russell sent Roy a one-way train ticket to join the New Orleans-rooted band at the Savoy Ballroom in Harlem just after Labor Day. Roy was twenty years old for his first New York gig.

He stayed with Russell for several years, improving his technique. "I was young and sort of flashy at the time. I had a special number with the band." Roy enjoyed his good paycheck, too. With the band, he made one of his first recordings, a hit version of the old standard "The Very Thought of You" on the Apollo label. And he made the rounds of the first-rate theaters in the African-American entertainment world at that

Roy Haynes

time—the Royal in Baltimore, the Regal in Chicago, the Earle in Philadelphia, the Paradise in Detroit, and the Howard in Washington.

His hero was Jo Jones, whom he first heard at the RKO theater in Boston. Roy's brother had introduced him to Jo, who called him "young talent" and "you little chuckle head." "He was the father of the drummers who play on that style. We all loved Sid Catlett. A lot of us didn't

get a chance to see Chick Webb in person, but we knew all about him
and his records such as 'Liza.' I loved all the great drummers—Cozy
Cole, and I could name people forever."

Roy joined tenor saxophonist Lester Young in 1947 at the Savoy in
Harlem and stayed with him for two years, until Lester went with Jazz
at the Philharmonic. Then Roy went to 52nd Street to play with small
groups led by Miles Davis and Bird in 1949.

"I played with Bird at Cafe Society Downtown. We appeared there for
four weeks opposite [the master pianist] Art Tatum beginning in July
1950. Playing with Parker opposite Tatum! That was the most glorious
five weeks of my musical career up to then." One night Billie Holiday sang
with them, and another time dancer Roy Bolger did a soft shoe. The club
was packed—and hot. Bird's group wore suits and ties. Although there
was no air conditioning, the music was so wonderful that Roy never left
the club even on the breaks. A man who would always love beautiful cars,
he bought his first new car in that period—a rocket engine 98 Oldsmobile.

He met his wife, Lee, when he was playing with Miles at a Brooklyn
club. They married in the 1950s; among their children, two sons grew up
to be musicians—Graham, a cornetist, and Craig, a drummer. Their daughter, Leslie Caren Haynes, married a saxophonist in the gospel music world.
Roy loved to recall how he sat in his car during an intermission from his gig
at the Five Spot with Monk and listened to a famous jazz disk jockey
announce Leslie's birth and her weight on the radio. "So it was an up."

Frequently, as he grew older, Roy liked to walk or drive around in
areas of Manhattan where he had once played and lived, before he
moved to Queens. "There's a lot of history and memories in me. I played
with Sarah, Ella, Billie, and with Louis Armstrong in 1946, and with
Coltrane, Monk, Eric Dolphy, Chick Corea, guitarist Pat Metheny. I
don't mean for one day, not just sitting in. No. 'I've Covered the Water-
front.' I considered myself one of them, Bird and the others."

Roy formed his own group, the Hip Ensemble, in 1969 and kept
leading it, with changing personnel, into the 1990s. He named albums he

had been proud of through the years: *Out of the Afternoon* on Impulse done in 1962; *We Three* with pianist Phineas Newborn and bassist Paul Chambers; and an album called *Blues for Coltrane* with an all-star group that earned a collective Grammy. Another album done with bassist Miroslav Vitous and pianist Chick Corea was nominated for a Grammy. Other albums included, in the 1990s, *When It Haynes, It Roars*, on Dreyfus, a French label; the Evidence album, *Homecoming*, done live in Sculler's, a Boston club, in 1994; and *Te Vou*, on the Dreyfus label in 1995. They earned critical praise.

When he hired youngsters to play, he observed the way they listened to music, how they played, what they said, and how they blended with the group on stage. Sometimes Roy pushed his group hard. Young saxophonist Ralph Moore told him that he learned a lot from Roy's drive. "He described me as one of the guys on a team. I throw a pass way ahead of time, and it lands, and he has to anticipate where it is landing. I learned about myself from hearing what Ralph Moore said."

For inspiration, Roy listened for anything that he could relate to, something that might take him in a new direction—"something warm to touch me," he said. He loved listening to old records by the masters. "The melody is always there, and it's not always there with the newer players. To know the melody is very important even if you don't play it. I hear newer players who don't know the correct notes, and there's something lost. My favorites to listen to are Art Tatum, Coleman Hawkins, Bird, Coltrane. I like to listen to all of them. The older stuff makes me feel comfortable." By newer players, he didn't necessarily mean young players but anyone he hadn't heard of before.

He was very excited just before going to receive an award in California and play with musicians whom he had never played with before. He said, "I got rhythm . . . in the name of the Lord. . . . Keep your ears open. We're going to get you. The rhythm is going to get you—tonight! I feel good. If I don't sound good, it's not my fault."

THE COOL SCHOOL

The cool school began with Gil Evans, a very important, California-born arranger and keyboardist who fell in love with Duke Ellington's harmonies and voicings and took his lessons learned by ear into the swing era band of Claude Thornhill. Evans also loved the sound of Miles Davis's trumpet first recorded in hard-driving bebop bands. By the late 1940s, Evans was living in New York, where his studio became a headquarters for jazz musicians—Miles Davis and baritone saxophonist and arranger Gerry Mulligan among them.

They organized a nonet and played a cool, less frenetic music than bebop. Miles was sick of the thicket of chords in bebop. And for his haunting sound in the middle register of the trumpet, the cooler approach of Evans's and Mulligan's arrangements was very well suited. An excellent example of the style was a song called "Boplicity," co-composed by Miles and Gil and recorded by Miles on April 22, 1949, as part of an album called *Birth of the Cool*. Kenny Clarke played drums for that album.

Leaving New York, Gerry Mulligan went to California in the early 1950s. There he became both famous and solvent for organizing a quartet and recording with it. The music, with a vibrato-less and cool tone, popularized the California sound. It may have been inspired to begin with by the laid-back lifestyle and beach culture of California. In any case, the sound of Mulligan's group was pared down, without a piano. The front line was made up of Mulligan and Chet Baker, a young trumpeter who would become known as a very bad boy in the jazz world—a stone junkie. But, miraculously defying the odds, he managed to remain a star for most of his life because of his beautiful, perfectly tuned, balanced, and poignant sound as a trumpeter and a singer.

The bassist in Mulligan's group was Red Mitchell; the drummer was Chico Hamilton. Their first recordings were done as private tapings by a man named Richard Bock, who realized they were so good that he started a little company, the Pacific Jazz label, to distribute them.

Born on September 21, 1921, in Los Angeles, **Chico Hamilton** was stunned the first time he saw Sonny Greer at the top of the pyramid of the Duke Ellington orchestra. Greer had "more drums than a drum shop,"[6] Hamilton would recall. Sonny became Chico's first great inspiration. Later Jo Jones became Chico's idol. Over time, Chico formulated his philosophy of music, which is that the rhythm, the beat, and not the melody, is the universal language of man. Maturing at a time when a search for new sounds dominated the jazz world, he embodied the California style in groups with careful arrangements and unusual, even eccentric instrumentation. Cool jazz groups often used cellos and French horns.

In grammar school, he began playing clarinet. One of his brothers played drums in the grade school band. When that brother graduated and went to another school, Chico decided he would replace him on drums. "I didn't know a thing about them. I fooled around. I got into them, and they got into me," he would recall. In his teen years he studied drums with Lee Young. By his mid-teens, he was playing in varied groups for little gigs in town. He was even sought out by Duke Ellington to sit in for two weeks for Sonny Greer in a Los Angeles theater.

Then the Gerry Mulligan quartet boosted his reputation in 1952 and 1953. He met Mulligan in New York first, then again in Los Angeles, when Gerry arrived to play in the studios. "He was having a rough time, a down period. He used to come in the joint where I was playing and hang out. I'd buy him a drink. We became friends." In that period, Chico was playing in a band for Lena Horne. But he decided to stay in Los Angeles at the time Gerry started a quartet. "As far as I'm concerned, we happened to be four people together at the right place at the right time. . . . That's when something really happens musically. . . . Harmonically and rhythmically, musicians make music, and it's happening. . . .

"It was very good. At first he didn't want me to use a bass drum, but I couldn't take it. So I took a tom-tom and converted it to a little bass drum. I was identified with that. And I was the first to use bottomless heads. I got a citation from [New York] Governor Hugh Carey for com-

Chico Hamilton at the 1956 Newport Jazz Festival

ing up with that idea. It was a matter of logic. During the war, before drumheads became plastic, they were made from calfskins. And during the war, we couldn't get them. So, to preserve my heads, I took them off the bottom. They lasted longer. When they frayed, I replaced them. I reached the point where I started digging the sound. And that was it." He also became known for playing with mallets and brushes instead of sticks.

He, too, recorded with his own group for the Pacific label; the first album was called Trio, with bassist George Duvivier and guitarist Howard Roberts. In later albums, Chico used a guitar, flute, clarinet, alto sax, cello, bass, and drums. He was criticized for his unorthodox emphasis on strings in a jazz group. But the Chico Hamilton Quintet with its swing, lightness, confidence, and striking voicings became a star of the Newport Jazz Festival in 1956. He took Eric Dolphy, a struggling young reeds player who would become lionized for his adventurous and beautiful ideas for free jazz, into the band. Chico's band gave Dolphy greater exposure and helped introduce him to important musicians and critics on the East Coast.

Later Chico led a group for the soundtrack of the film entitled *The Sweet Smell of Success*. He also wrote "The Morning After," a song for that film. CBS heard it when the company had the Gerald McBoing-Boing series, and they used Chico's song as the theme. Next, he was in London working with Lena Horne, when he was asked to score the film *Repulsion* for Roman Polansky, whom Chico met through a mutual friend. In New York, he did a commercial for the prestigious Grey Advertising Agency. "It was very successful, and it was well-paid work. I said to myself, 'To get that much money, I should come back to New York and start a company.'" So he did. He spent the 1960s and 1970s earning a great deal of money from the advertising business. With his profits, he built a luxurious country house for his family on Long Island. He also led fusion groups and tried to fight prejudice against electric instruments in the mainstream, acoustic, bebop-happy jazz world of New York beginning in the 1960s. Eventually he would teach at the New School in New York. And he began to work on a book of autobiographical essays with the witty title *The Skin You Love to Touch*. When he disengaged himself from the advertising business, he put a group together and started touring. "Fortunately my name hadn't been off the scene. They treat me like a superstar in Japan and Europe."

"I can't stress enough that I feel blessed. It took me a long time to start to teach, and I didn't know if I'd dig it." Before the first semester was over, he knew that by teaching he could give something back to his craft. Music had been so good to him, he felt, that he owed it to music to teach. One of the things he teaches young musicians is that the work isn't always very well paid. "Some days you can't get arrested. That's dealing with the culture of the arts . . . I teach not only rhythm, but pride in being a musician, and how important it is to be a professional, because it will pay off. If nothing else happens, you can always rejoice in how you can play or listen to music." He doesn't, however, teach musicians the business or management end of their work, because, he says, "Making a living in the street teaches musicians what they do and don't do. It's no different than dealing with any other career, whether it's high finance or politics. You learn the hard way."

He decorated his studio with his awards; he placed consistently in the Drummers and Jazz Electric Combos categories in the popularity polls in *Down Beat* magazine. The Mexican government honored him for doing benefits and charities. One award, which an American corporation gave him for a film score, looks like a crystal wedding cake sculpted inside glass. It sits on a shelf in his studio in Manhattan. "My awards, or rewards, are the fact that I'm still able to play music—and THINK. Young players keep playing with me. They find me. And I'm going to keep playing. . . ."

THIRD STREAM MUSIC

Among the other heirs of the bebop revolution were musicians who pursued a close relationship with European music. Their experiments were dubbed Third Stream Music to connote the blending of the first stream, or European classical music, with the second stream, or the African-American jazz tradition. Third Stream Music developed when jazz became a concert music—music for listening, not especially for dancing—after World War II. All the elements of jazz became more sophisticated. Not all the Third Stream groups were successful; some were too intellectual and had no ability to excite listeners.

The most successful Third Stream group was the *Modern Jazz Quartet* (MJQ). The group was formed by pianist John Lewis, who was trained in classical music, swinging vibraphonist Milt Jackson, bassist Percy Heath, and drummer Kenny Clarke. *Connie Kay* replaced Clarke in 1955.

The group disbanded for a while in 1974 when it couldn't find enough bookings at its financial and professional level during the reign of rock music. But it began playing again in the 1980s and continued full strength into the 1990s. Lewis and Jackson were the featured players in the quartet, while Heath and Kay provided excellent support. Connie Kay was meticulous and driving, able to wrest perfect tones from his drums and cymbals to embellish and strengthen the sound of the whole group.

The Modern Jazz Quartet (left to right): John Lewis, Percy Heath, Connie Kay, and Milt Jackson

He would recall how he was called by the MJQ manager one day in 1955 to see if he would go along for a concert in Washington, D.C., then a gig in Storyville in Boston, for two weeks altogether. John Lewis filled Kay in about one of the group's staple songs, "Django," as they traveled by train to Washington. Kay played the two weeks, and "when it was over, nobody said anything and nobody has yet and that was thirty years ago," he later said.[8] Kay fit right in with the MJQ format.

Kay adored Sid Catlett. He was working after school and on Saturdays at a Chinese art gallery in the East 50s in Manhattan when he first heard Catlett. Kay passed the club Cafe Society Uptown between Lexington and Park Avenues on 58th Street. With the door open, Big Sid was rehearsing there with Teddy Wilson's band. Later, Kay, with his old Studebaker car, offered Catlett a ride home to Harlem after another club date. They became friends and went to hear music together in clubs.

Kay was fascinated by Catlett's versatility. Catlett could play with any kind of group, from Dixieland to bebop or show music for chorus girls; he could play solo and rivet the attention of a crowd. "He taught me little things," Connie recalled. "He'd stop by where I was working and tell me my left hand was too inactive or my beat on the ride cymbal was too loud, and he'd show me things at his house. But I learned the most from him in his attitude—his quiet, beautiful way toward things, whether it was the world situation or just people."[8] Unlike Catlett, Kay would never like to take solos and preferred a supportive role in groups.

Born in April 1927, Connie Kay was the only child of West Indian immigrants from the island of Montserrat. His mother played piano and organ in church, and his father played the guitar. But Connie preferred to take wooden bars out of coat hangers, shape them into drumsticks, and play on the hassock in the house. He had a friend with a snare drum, and they used to play that together. Kay simply loved drums. He began playing professionally by taking little jobs in New York, and one job led to another and to tours.

By the 1950s, he could get a job with anyone. He knew his strength lay in his excellent timekeeping abilities. He made rock and roll records for Atlantic Records. He played with Lester Young on and off for five or six years. Then came the gig with the MJQ, which assured him a prominent, venerated place in jazz history.

When the MJQ was formed, its music sounded revolutionary, ethereal, almost like music from outer space. Eventually it came to sound familiar, soothing, and even very measured and conservative. In the mid-1950s the band began recording. In 1960, in Stockholm, Sweden, it recorded *European Concert*, an album on the Atlantic label and probably the band's best album. It included fine versions of the MJQ's best originals, including "Django" by John Lewis and Milt Jackson's "Bags' Groove." The group stayed together for so long that the music they played became repetitious for Connie. But nobody played the same thing exactly the same way twice, he said. Lewis might write out a drum part but allowed Connie to change it. And he had complete freedom behind the soloists. He could feel when they were about to end a solo or had run out of what they wanted to do with a song. And he could feel when someone might want to change the rhythm or double the tempo. He simply knew how every one in the group was going to breathe.

Connie Kay died in 1994. The group tried to replace him with Percy Heath's brother, Tootie, a fine drummer.

From these groups and styles, jazz would evolve even more, as musicians always sought new sounds and ideas with which to express themselves and tantalize the public. But these players invented the classic, early modern jazz styles.

CHAPTER EIGHT

TONY WILLIAMS, ELVIN JONES, AND OTHER MASTERS OF MODERN DRUMMING

The history of jazz drumming—and jazz itself—in the 1960s and 1970s must take into account the political and social ferment in the United States.

The nation rejected the stodgy status quo of the Eisenhower era when, in 1960, the American people elected John F. Kennedy, a handsome young president with vision. He seemed to stand for social progress and self-expression. For one thing, he founded the Peace Corps, an inspiring concept that gave idealistic young Americans the opportunity to travel and help people improve their lives in underdeveloped countries.

During the early 1960s, the civil rights movement became increasingly active and successful. The March on Washington in 1963 symbolized the growing strength of the movement.

In other areas of their lives, Americans pushed against the boundaries of the status quo in social mores and lifestyles—including sexual relationships. People made their own choices about their lifestyles and didn't simply follow prescribed routes anymore.

In 1963, President Kennedy was assassinated. His successor, President Lyndon Baines Johnson, escalated a very unpopular, commercially motivated, and disastrous war waged by the United States in Vietnam. The United States was divided into hostile camps—those who supported the war, and those who protested against it vociferously. Public opinion was so strong against the war that President Johnson, despite his brilliant leadership for civil rights legislation, was forced to announce he wouldn't run for a second term in office. By then, many people distrusted the government and any related authority. Popular music reflected the country's restlessness and dissatisfaction. The music became loud, and it had a simple, elemental beat that allowed people to dance, shout, and let go of their inhibitions—in effect, to protest, seemingly about everything. Not only had John F. Kennedy been assassinated, but in 1968, so was his brother Senator Robert F. Kennedy, a presidential candidate, and the revered civil rights leader Martin Luther King, Jr. Folk, rock and roll, and rhythm and blues in the 1960s, then disco music in the 1970s, hypnotized the public. These loud styles acted as a kind of narcotic to dull the pain and perhaps even block out the complexities of modern life.

At the same time, jazz became increasingly abstract. In the late 1950s, alto saxophonist Ornette Coleman, bassist Charles Mingus, and pianist Cecil Taylor alarmed some of the jazz-loving public by introducing atonality into jazz compositions and performances. The musicians in the groups screeched on their instruments. The music sounded chaotic and upsetting. Iconoclastic and highly intellectualized, it, like rock, reflected social and political unrest. But abstract jazz had far fewer fans than rock, because abstract jazz was so much less comprehensible for most people. The experimental music was dubbed "free jazz."

A very small number of jazz fans and critics found the new music exciting. But for the most part, traditional jazz audiences walked out of the clubs—and into the audiences for popular music. Rock reigned as the commercially viable, emotionally expressive, popular music.

Though jazz went into commercial eclipse, several great group leaders developed fascinating musical concepts. Two of the most important were Miles Davis and John Coltrane. And the drummers in their groups helped to set standards for other drummers — both their contemporaries and youngsters yet to begin their careers.

Both Davis and Coltrane decided to leave behind the chords that were the emblem and mainstay of the bebop style. Instead the leaders used modes, an ancient musical invention, as the basis for their improvising. A mode is a sequence of notes that establishes a tonality or a keynote. With modes, jazz musicians found themselves less encumbered by the chords and freer to improvise melodies. Of course, the players needed good enough imaginations to work with modes and improvise varied music from them.

Modal music wasn't free jazz. But it was a freer style of jazz than bebop. And although Miles had criticized Ornette Coleman harshly, Miles's music would eventually become freer not only as a result of his own experiments but also because of Ornette's seemingly zany, iconoclastic, but tantalizing ideas. A new sense of freedom was in the air.

In Miles Davis's groups, Jimmy Cobb played drums for *Kind of Blue*, Miles's 1959 album. It demonstrated the haunting beauty soloists could achieve by improvising upon modes and around tonal centers. The deceptively simple tune "All Blues" from the album became beloved by musicians and audiences. It is played as one of the most important, easily recognizable modern jazz standards to this day. And Cobb had the ability to play with such tenderness and attentiveness to the melody that Sarah Vaughan, the great jazz diva, chose him to play in her trio for years beginning in the late 1960s.

Jimmy Cobb joined Miles as a replacement for Philly Joe Jones, an extremely creative, exciting, aggressive drummer. Jones was in and out of Miles Davis's group for years and led his own groups. Many drummers regarded Philly Joe, the drummer on Miles's album *Porgy and Bess*, as an inspiration and a role model for his imagination and playing abilities. Some critics have said that was Miles Davis's best album. Jimmy Cobb stayed with Miles until 1963, when he, the bassist Paul Chambers, and the pianist Wynton Kelly, who constituted Miles's rhythm section, left to work as a group themselves.

Jimmy Cobb

In 1963, modern drumming took a giant step forward when a young-ster named *Tony Williams* was hired to play in a Miles Davis group. Miles, by then the guru of his groups, often gave his young musicians mysterious directions. He "provoked Tony Williams's whipcrack sound on snare drum when he told the teenager to 'play that Rat Patrol stuff.' No one knew what he had in mind, nor did he explain. 'Rat Patrol,' it was discovered, was a television series about a tank battalion. . . . Miles was requesting a more martial drum sound. He got Tony off the cym-bals-with-brushes behind the horns, the way everybody else played, and onto the snare-with-sticks," the group's pianist Herbie Hancock said. "It gave us a whole new sound."[1] *'Four' & More*, an album led by Miles and taped at a benefit performance for the Congress of Racial Equality on the Columbia label in 1964, is powered by Tony Williams's exuberant fills, and the rhythm section "crackles beneath Miles on every track."[2]

Tony, at age seventeen in 1963, was discovered in a Boston club by alto saxophonist Jackie McLean, who invited Tony to play in his group in New York. There Miles Davis came to the club with Philly Joe Jones, who admired Williams's playing. A month later, in May 1963, Miles called Tony to join his group. Tony stayed for about five years. In that group, he developed his imagination more than ever, his explosive power, and his great skills.

He made many of Miles's most important albums in the 1960s, and he went on to play on other exceptional records such as Herbie Hancock's *Maiden Voyage* and *Speak Like a Child*, as well as *V.S.O.P.: the Quintet*, the name of one of V.S.O.P.'s albums. Eventually Tony led his own groups, which his sidemen viewed as a great chance to learn from a masterful leader.

Growing up in an age of electronics, electric instruments, and rock music, he gravitated toward using electronic equipment to help him develop his music. He told interviewer Herb Wong for *Jazz Times* magazine in September 1988, "The emotional content of my playing is one thing that's never missing—passion, emotion and aggressive playing—these three things make up most of what I do. It's drumming. It's not bass playing. That's why I write the way I do. Drummers have certain kinds of bands. . . . I'm a drummer and I must have a certain type of music, which is why I'm also attracted to pop music and, of course, rock 'n' roll allows a bigger beat. Playing with a lot of power can be attractive to a drummer and I accept the fact that a jazz bassist or keyboardist may not understand that.

"The things that are in flux include mainly my technique. It's the one thing that's changing because of my changing ideas. I play differently now than some years ago. I try to get ideas from varied sources; e.g., a drum machine will give me new ideas, since you can program something you've never played before. . . ."[3]

Williams also thought his drumming had changed because he was older. And "drums to me are super dynamic. I enjoy playing the full scope of the instrument. To not play loud on the drums is like telling a bass player he can only play on three strings when he's got four to use, or telling a pianist to play only in the middle register — that he can't play down in the bottom or at the top. So playing loud is really like playing soft, as you can then hear and appreciate the true dynamics. When you get soft then, it truly means something. . . ." Williams also stressed that he loved interacting with people in his band; he didn't like playing in a vacuum. He had learned, even before joining Miles, the importance of give and take, and he had already begun filling gaps where people weren't playing.

"I studied each drummer I liked and listened to intently, to determine what they were and were not doing individually, identifying their tendencies — all kinds of jazz drummers, Louis Hayes, Jimmy Cobb . . . Roy Brooks, Ed Thigpen [who played with such groups as master pianist Oscar Peterson's], Roy Haynes and Connie Kay, for instance . . . this analysis helped me to move beyond what I was doing — which was doing what everyone else was doing, and I sounded like everybody — but then I started doing them in different places, different contexts and contributing to my own sound. I still may sound like Max's or Blakey's sounds . . . however, if I began playing what Max would . . . sound like for a minute, I'll follow with playing like Roy Haynes because Max has never played like that; then I might do something reminiscent of Louis Hayes or Ginger Baker."

In short, Williams developed his style by blending the techniques and styles of his forerunners and contemporaries. It's important to note how much Williams says he likes rock drumming for its big beat. Every drummer from the 1960s on would be influenced by the loudness of rock music. And audiences would adore and encourage that loudness. It was the antithesis, to older jazz fans, of the essence of jazz, originally an art stressing the beauty of an intimate sound. But fusion jazz combining electric and acoustic instruments and rock itself were much louder styles of music. The increased decibel level of modern jazz was an innovation in itself—and an important, aesthetic development for modern popular music. Young people loved loud music. Since they were the ones who bought records, went to clubs and concerts, their tastes prevailed. They got what they wanted.

Tenor saxophonist John Coltrane had a great impact on jazz after 1960. In many ways he was more influential than Miles, although Miles would become better known than any other modern acoustic jazz musician. Coltrane had a thorough understanding of chord progressions. But in 1960 he moved on to modal improvising on the soprano and tenor saxophones. And he devoted himself to presenting moral and spiritual uplift through his music. For his groups, he hired drummer *Elvin Jones*, who, with his own tremendous energy, contributed to Coltrane's intensity. Coltrane was famous for playing constantly both on and off stage and seemed to have a boundless supply of energy.

Elvin stayed with Coltrane from 1960 to 1966, developing his loose, creative, and free style of drumming. "During my time with Coltrane, I could investigate my quest of how to play with other instruments," Elvin told Whitney Balliett.[4] "He left me absolutely alone. He must have felt the way I played, understood the validity of it. There was never any rhythmic or melodic or harmonic conflicts. At least I never felt any . . . I was never conscious of the length of Coltrane's solos, which sometimes lasted forty minutes. I was in the position of being able to follow his melodic line through all the modes he would weave in and out of, through all the patterns and the endless variations on variations. It was like listening to a concerto. The only thing that mattered was the completion of the cycle that he was in. . . .

"I didn't want to leave Coltrane, but the personnel had changed. He added another drummer, and I couldn't hear what I was doing any

Elvin Jones

longer. . . . In those last weeks I had a constant migraine headache." (A year later, in 1967, Coltrane died. Many people believed he had simply worn himself out.)

Elvin Jones, a younger brother of pianist Hank and trumpeter Thad, both of them stars in the jazz world, never considered playing any instrument but drums. He studied and loved the bebop masters Kenny Clarke and Max Roach, and the even older masters Chick Webb, Jo Jones, and

Baby Dodds. Beginning his drumming education, he listened to parade drummers, circus bands, even the American Legion Drum Corps. He played with many fine musicians in Detroit from 1949 on.

Elvin began playing as a child by learning to count and by studying all twenty-six rudiments in his drum instruction book. In school, his band director "made me realize that the drum is not something to bang on, that it is not a round disc to be pounded. He told me you can hear incoherent sounds in a traffic jam and that music should go far beyond the production of traffic jams."[5] He listened to his family's collection of records and learned to play along with them. The experience taught him, most of all, how valuable it is to keep time, and that timekeeping is the drummer's primary function.

He named all the well-known swing-era and bebop drummers as his greatest influences. "I began to develop my theories on drums. I figured that a lot of things drummers were doing with two hands could be done with one—like accents with just the left hand on the snare, so you wouldn't have to take your right hand off the ride cymbal. And it didn't seem to me that the four-four beat on the bass drum was necessary. What was needed was a *flow* of rhythm all over the set. I never learned any tricks, anything flashy—like juggling sticks or throwing them in the air. That kind of thing stops me inside. After all, Arthur Rubinstein doesn't play runs on the piano with his chin. . . ."[6]

"My drums are my life," Elvin said, and he explained some of his technique. "Playing is a matter of spontaneity *and* thought, of constant control. Take a solo. When I start, I keep the structure and melody and content of the tune in my mind and work up abstractions or obligatos on it . . . I can see forms and shapes in my mind, when I solo, just as a painter can see forms and shapes when he starts painting. And I can see different colors. My cymbals will be one color and my snare another color and my tom-toms each a different color. I mix these colors up, making constant movement. Drums suggest movement, a conscious, constant shifting of sounds and levels of sound. My drumming can shade from a whisper to a thunder."[7]

Sometimes he takes very long solos. Balliett described a performance by Jones—his constantly shifting beat, his wholly unpredictable bass drum accents, his use of all parts of his drum set in unexpected ways, with the total effect of an unbroken flow that both supported and wove itself around the soloists. And for his solo, he played complex, abstract, loud, and engulfing rhythms. The audience could not take its eyes off him.[8]

Jones is the epitome of the modern acoustic jazz drummer. He makes the rhythm flow all over the drum set and plays it as a percussionist does, for colors and accents, while never losing sight or control of his time-keeping responsibilities. No one can forget the spectacle of this powerfully built man ranging all over his drum set and ruling it; his performances are titanic.

After he left Coltrane's group and led his own very popular groups, he hired pianists and bassists who played electric instruments—though he thought people involved in electronics had to be very careful about how they used them and certainly should not do it just for the sake of making loud music.

To young drummers, he offered the advice: "Learn to roll: Learn how to make a perfect roll. . . . Try to be able to execute a five-minute roll. I think that would keep any young student busy for about two years!" he told Art Taylor for *Notes and Tones*.[9] He also advised players to develop control, which he believed was done primarily through long hours of practice and trial and error—practical experience.

There were other, very important drummers beginning in the 1960s in Miles's group. Master drummer *Jack DeJohnette*, who played in Miles Davis's group after Tony Williams, went on to win critics' polls for years as the greatest jazz drummer in the world, and to lead his own groups and nurture young musicians on all the instruments. DeJohnette can be heard on the Miles Davis album *Bitches Brew*, generally regarded as the first fusion album, on the Columbia label in 1969. With fusion, Miles was able to call attention to jazz and interest young listeners accustomed to the loudness of rock.

Billy Higgins, revered for his great imagination and technique, has played for many years with pianist Cedar Walton's mainstream acoustic groups and can be heard on many albums with Cedar. But Higgins is also renowned for his work in free jazz groups, because he can play without ties to a demanding beat, and he enjoys his liberation to pursue a variety of accent patterns. Higgins played for the revolutionary album, so controversial in its time — Ornette Coleman's *The Shape of Jazz to Come* on the Atlantic label in 1959. For Coleman's album *Free Jazz* in 1960, also on Atlantic, the drummer was *Ed Blackwell*, another early star of the free jazz style or movement. New Orleans-born Blackwell went on to have an illustrious career, playing with important free jazz musicians and teaching at Wesleyan University.

Billy Higgins

Among other drummers noted for their work in free jazz and experimental groups are **Dannie Richmond**, who played with the mercurial, demanding bassist, composer, and creative genius Charles Mingus. Mingus's inspired work approaches free jazz. **Andrew Cyrille** recorded for the exceptionally iconoclastic pianist Cecil Taylor's *Unit Structures* on Blue Note in 1967. **Famoudou Don Moye**, a multi-percussion instrumentalist, recorded with the extremely eccentric Art Ensemble of Chicago, a group formed in the 1960s to play music which is still, like Cecil Taylor's, definitely an acquired taste for most listeners. Percussionist **Colin Walcott** powered the group Oregon. And drummer **Rashied Ali** led his own groups.

These interesting drummers fascinated a small percentage of jazz fans at first. The musicians had to find their rewards strictly in their artistic achievements. With their courage leading them, they persisted in their experiments as percussionists and soloists.

At the other end of the spectrum, in fusion jazz and pop groups in the 1970s and 1980s, were the drummers in **Weather Report**, which had hits with songs such as "Birdland," and the **Yellowjackets,** with its hit "The Spin," and **Spyro Gyra** with its familiar "Morning Dance," to name a few representative groups. Their happy-sounding, easily understood tunes captured the public's fancy.

Several Brazilian percussionists have made their mark in jazz. Best known have been Airto Morera, who has played with Miles Davis, Weather Report, and Return to Forever. He also leads groups starring his wife, Brazilian singer Flora Purira.

Nana Vasconcelos is probably the most exciting and virtuostic *berimbau* player ever heard in the United States. An exotic instrument made from a gourd and string, the berimbau sings miraculously in Nana's hands. He and Airto add exoticism to North American jazz groups with their unusual instruments for percussion and special effects.

All these styles of music had an effect on an emerging generation of mainstream acoustic jazz musicians who, when they began playing as students, had no idea that they would mature as acoustic jazz players.

Most of them thought they would have careers in rock and roll or rhythm and blues or fusion. Otherwise, they knew, they ran the risk of starving to death. But in the late 1970s and 1980s, a variety of events breathed life back into the mainstream acoustic jazz world.

Rock concerts became dangerous, and parents didn't want their children to attend them. The kids became fascinated with video games, while older people looked around for another, more sophisticated form of entertainment. Record companies, hoping to fill the void left by rock concerts, reissued old acoustic jazz albums—by Miles, among others. And the public began to buy them.

Then Columbia Records took the chance of signing Wynton Marsalis, a handsome young trumpeter who could play both jazz and classical music. His records sold in great numbers, and young people bought tickets to his concerts and club appearances, too. Excited by Wynton's success, other record companies signed many young musicians in the hope of finding more Wyntons playing all the instruments.

Then new technology convinced people to invest in expensive audio equipment and buy jazz on compact discs. And record companies began converting much of their music on long playing records to compact discs.

Clubs featuring acoustic jazz opened and attracted customers. In New York City's Greenwich Village, scores of clubs existed within walking distance of one another. One young acoustic drummer, ***Marvin "Smitty" Smith***, was brought to New York by singer Jon Hendricks and his group in December 1981 to play in a new club, Lush Life. Smitty had been attending the Berklee School of Music in Boston, and he was immersed in jazz drumming traditions. When Smitty, still in his late teens in 1981, reached New York, he was overjoyed at the amount of jazz he heard around him. Furthermore, wherever he sat in, people loved to hear him play. Within a very short time, he found himself invited to work in the groups of many older musicians who themselves were finding high-profile gigs at decent fees for the first time in years. He knew the timekeeping traditions, and he also had a brilliant imagination for improvisations.

From all over the country, young musicians began to arrive on the scene in New York. Some of them played in Wynton Marsalis's groups, and others simply popped up in the best jazz clubs, hired by older players. Then, increasingly, as the older players retired or died, the youngsters led their own groups or played in groups led by their contemporaries. Drummer Kenny Washington, immersed in jazz history, found he could play every night of the week, if he chose, with fine leaders. He became one of the most tasteful and popular sidemen on drums. Dennis Mackrell, a drummer with the astounding ability to swing a big band, showed up in trumpeter and arranger Buck Clayton's band in the 1980s. Clayton had been a star in Count Basie's first band that had formed in Kansas City in the 1930s. Mackrell went on to play for the Basie band when it was led by musicians who inherited its leadership after Basie's death. Among many other drummers who became prominent during the renaissance of jazz in the 1980s and 1990s have been Lewis Nash and Victor Lewis, whose presence in any group attracts audiences.

Another surprising phenomenon occurred in the jazz world. Women drummers began to get chances to play in groups in first-rate clubs and concert halls. Until the 1980s, jazz had been virtually an all-male preserve. It was the rare woman who ever got a chance to play an instrument in a prominent position. But the rock star then known as Prince hired percussionist Sheila E, and audiences started to become used to the sight of a woman playing percussion. Even Miles Davis hired a woman percussionist for a concert at Carnegie Hall in the mid-1980s.

Terri Lyne Carrington, long known in the jazz world as a child prodigy on the drum set, found jobs with famous jazz groups as she grew up in the 1980s. By mid-decade, she became the first drummer to play in the group for Arsenio Hall's late night talk show. But she disliked the confining world of the studios, and she went on the road again in groups led by Stan Getz and singer Al Jarreau. Based in Los Angeles, she moved back and forth from rock and roll to acoustic jazz, one of several women drummers who could find challenging and well-paid work during the renaissance of the public's interest in jazz.

Terri Lyne Carrington

Another was Sherrie Maricle, who played with the New York Pops Orchestra led by Skitch Henderson. She helped organize Diva, an all-women's band that earned critical acclaim in the 1990s and used, for its slogan, No Man's Band. Sylvia Cuerica sat in with veteran Clark Terry's group in the Village Vanguard one night. And Terry hired her for his group. Composer and drummer Cindy Blackman has recorded as a leader for Muse Records and moves back and forth from the jazz to the pop music scene in prominent groups.

All these drummers combined a wealth of influences — the originality and respect for timekeeping of the great old jazz drummers, the adventurousness and sophistication of the beboppers and post-beboppers, and the courage of the free jazz experimenters, along with the freedom of the rock and rollers to make themselves heard as a powerful force to excite and overwhelm audiences. No longer did recording technicians even dream of muffling drums. Instead, rock and fusion drummers sometimes even use two bass drums in their sets, so advanced is the technology and so accepting has the public become of the spell of the drums, whether played softly or at a near-deafening level. As Art Blakey said about the importance of drummers, "The drummer is the one who interprets everything and puts it together."[10]

SOURCE NOTES

CHAPTER ONE

1. Len Lyons, *The 101 Best Jazz Albums* (New York: William Morrow, 1980), p. 19.

2. Marshall W. Stearns, *The Story of Jazz* (New York: Oxford University Press, 1956, 1958, and revised and in paperback, 1970), p. 61–62.

3. Baby Dodds, as told to Larry Gara, *The Baby Dodds Story*, revised edition (Baton Rouge: Louisiana State University Press, 192), p. 39.

4. Barry Kernfeld, editor, *The New Grove Dictionary of Jazz* (New York: St. Martin's Press, 1995), p. 308–309.

CHAPTER TWO

1. All direct and paraphrased quotes from Lewis come from this radio series, which is not published or commercially available.

2. *The Baby Dodds Story*, p. 55.

3. All direct and paraphrased quotes from Lewis come from this radio series, which is not published or commercially available.

4. *The New Grove Dictionary of Jazz*, p. 313.

CHAPTER THREE

1. *The Baby Dodds Story*, p. 3.

2. Ibid., p. 6.

3. Ibid., p. 9.

4. Ibid., p. 23.

5. Ibid., p. 25.

6. Ibid., p. 27.

7. Ibid., pp. 31–32.

8. Ibid., pp. 33.

9. Ibid., pp. 37–38.

10. Ibid., p. 38.

11. Ibid., pp. 39–40.

12. Ibid., pp. 46–47.

13. Ibid., pp. 63–64.

CHAPTER FOUR

1. WKCR series with Mel Lewis and Loren Schoenberg.

2. Ibid.

3. Ibid.

4. Edward Berger, *Bassically Speaking: An Oral History of George Duvivier* (Metuchen, NJ: Rutgers, the State University of New Jersey, and the Scarecrow Press, 1993), p. 136.

5. WKCR series.

6. Burt Korall, *Drummin' Men* (New York: Schirmer Books, 1990), p. 102.

7. WKCR series.

8. Whitney Balliett, *American Musicians: 56 Portraits in Jazz* (New York: Oxford University Press, 1986), p. 123.

9. Ibid., p.124.

10. Ibid.

11. Ibid., p. 125.

12. Ibid., p. 56.

13. John Edward Hasse, *Beyond Category: The Life and Genius of Duke Ellington* (New York: Simon & Schuster, 1993), p. 161.

14. Ron Spagnardi, *The Great Jazz Drummers* (Cedar Grove, NJ: Modern Drummer Publications, 1992), p. 11.

15. *Drummin' Men*, p. 317.

16. George T. Simon, *The Big Bands*, fourth edition (New York: Schirmer Books, 1981), p. 440.

17. WKCR series.

18. *American Musicians: 56 Portraits in Jazz*, p. 183.

19. Conversation with drummer and jazz history expert Kenny Washington.

20. Ibid.

21. *Drummin' Men*, p. 49.

22. *The Big Bands*, p. 307.

23. Ibid.

24. *Drummin' Men*, p. 87.

25. *The Big Bands*, p. 311.

26. *Drummin' Men*, p. 250.

27. *American Musicians: 56 Portraits in Jazz*, p. 230.

28. Ibid., p. 231.

29. Ibid., p. 232.

30. Ibid., p. 233.

31. Ibid., p. 234.

32. Ibid.

CHAPTER FIVE

1. Arthur Taylor, *Notes and Tones* (New York: Perigee, 1977), p. 189.

2. Ibid., p. 192

3. Geoffrey Haydon and Dennis Marks, editors, *Repercussions: A Celebration of African-American Music* (London: Century Publishing, London, 1985), p. 77.

4. Ibid., p. 85.

5. Ibid., p. 86

6. *Notes and Tones*, pp. 108–109.

THE JAZZ DRUMMING TREE

1. Many of the ideas for this chapter were culled from *The New Grove Dictionary of Jazz*'s section on drums.

2. *The 101 Best Jazz Albums*, p. 97.

3. On the WKCR series on drumming, Mel Lewis refers to himself as a "bebopper."

4. *Notes and Tones*, p. 249–250.

CHAPTER SIX

Information on Cuban music was provided in a private lesson by Mario Bauza with the author in 1983. Information on Ray Mantilla comes from an interview by the author with Mr. Mantilla.

CHAPTER SEVEN

1. *Notes and Tones*, p. 239.

2. Dizzy Gillespie with Al Fraser, *To Be or Not to Bop* (New York: Doubleday, 1979), p. 194.

3. Ibid., p. 196.

4. *The 101 Best Jazz Albums*, p. 192.

5. From the author's interview with Roy Haynes in January 1995, shortly before his seventieth birthday. All quotes come from the interview with Haynes.

6. From the author's interviews with Chico Hamilton in New York in February 1995, before his seventy-fifth birthday in September. All quotes from Hamilton come from those interviews.

7. *American Musicians: 56 Portraits in Jazz*, p. 241.

8. Ibid., p. 244, with corroborating material from the author's conversations with Connie Kay.

CHAPTER EIGHT

1. *The 101 Best Jazz Albums*, p. 265.

2. Ibid.

3. Herb Wong, "World Class Drummer, Tony Williams," *Jazz Times* magazine (September 1988).

4. *American Musicians: 56 Portraits in Jazz*, p. 364.

5. Ibid., p. 369.

6. Ibid., p. 370.

7. Ibid., p. 371.

8. Ibid., p. 364.

9. *Notes and Tones*, pp. 228–229.

10. Ibid., p. 246.

SUGGESTED LISTENING

The availability of CDs changes fairly often, but some CDs are classics and always available in one form or another. The years when the music was recorded and the years of reissue are generally listed here if they have been included on the CD covers. The recordings appear in approximately the chronological order of their first release or else as representative of styles covered in this book.

Baby Dodds and Zutty Singleton

Louis Armstrong: The Hot Fives, Vol. 1; *The Hot Fives and Sevens*, Vols. 1 and 2, 1988; Vol. 3, Columbia Jazz Masterpieces, 1989.

Chick Webb

Spinnin' the Webb, Decca Jazz, 1996.

Chick Webb and His Orchestra, 1929–1934 and 1935–1938, Classics.

Buddy Rich

This One's for Basie, arrangements by Marty Paich, Verve Records, 1956.

The Best Band I Ever Had, DCC Jazz, 1977.

Very Live at Buddy's Place, Beast Retro, Pickwick Records, 1997.

Buddy Rich, Compact Jazz, Verve.

Mercy, Mercy, Pacific Jazz.

West Side Story, Laserlight, 1991.

Gene Krupa

Compact Jazz, with Gene Krupa, Anita O'Day, Roy Eldridge, Ben Webster, Teddy Wilson, Lionel Hampton, and others; contains "Drummin' Man," "Let Me Off Uptown," and others, Verve.

Uptown, Roy Eldridge, Anita O'Day, and Gene Krupa, Columbia.

Drummer Man, the Gene Krupa Big Band, with O'Day and Eldridge; contains "Drum Boogie," "Let Me Off Uptown," "Rockin' Chair," and others, Verve, 1956.

Benny Goodman's *Live at Carnegie Hall*, January 16, 1938; includes Krupa on "Sing, Sing, Sing," Columbia.

Gene Krupa and Buddy Rich, with pianist Oscar Peterson, trumpeter Dizzy Gillespie, trumpeter Roy Eldridge, and tenor saxophonist Flip Phillips, Verve, 1955.

Papa Jo Jones

Count Basie: The Complete Decca Recordings, a three-disc set, Decca, 1937–1939.

Count Basie: The Golden Years, featuring singers Helen Humes and Jimmy Rushing with drummer Jo Jones, Jazz Archives, EPM, 1938.

Count Basie: The Quintessence, a two-disc set, Fremeaux, 1937–1941.

Count Basie and His Orchestra, Classics, 1938–1939.

Count Basie and His Orchestra, recorded in 1942, reissued 1993.

The Essential Jo Jones, features Jones as leader, Vanguard, 1977.

Note: Any of the early Basie albums, 1930s and 1940s, features Jo Jones on drums. Also, in the 1950s, Basie had another excellent drummer, Sonny Payne, who can be heard on *The "Atomic" Band in Concert*, Bandstand, BDCD, Laserlight, circa 1955.

Ray McKinley

McKinley Time!; includes "The Celery Stalks at Midnight," P&C, Viper's Nest, 1996.

The Will Bradley-Ray McKinley Orchestra, from the Best of the Big Bands series, Aerospace,1940–1941.

Sonny Greer

Duke Ellington: The Blanton-Webster Band, RCA/Bluebird, 1986.

Duke Ellington and His Orchestra, Classics, 1928–1929.

Sonny Greer played and recorded with Duke until 1951.

Note: Among other interesting drummers who played with Duke was Louie Bellson, heard on Duke Ellington's *Black, Brown and Beige*, Music Masters Jazz, 1992. Bellson later recorded with his own group on such labels as Concord. Look for his solo performance of "Skin Deep" on a CD under his own name. Sam Woodyard was another drummer well known for his work in performances and on recordings with Ellington.

Kenny Clarke

Dizzy Gillespie, leader, *Shaw Nuff*, Musicraft, 1946.

Carmen McRae, leader, *By Special Request*, accompanied by the Mat Mathews Quintet including Clarke, Decca, 1954 or 1955.

Miles Davis, leader, *Walkin'*, Prestige.

The Giant, with Dizzy Gillespie, Accord, 1973.

Pieces of Time, with drummers and percussionists Famoudou Don Moye, Milford Graves, and Andrew Cyrille, Soul Note.

Max Roach

Now's the Time, with the Charlie Parker quartet, Drive.

Jazz at Massey Hall, originally on Debut, 1953, now a release on the Original Jazz Classics label; with pianist Bud Powell, trumpeter Dizzy Gillespie, bassist Charles Mingus, and alto saxophonist Charlie Parker.

Max Roach + 4, Emarcy, 1956 and 1957.

Clifford Brown and Max Roach, Jazz Masters 44, Verve, 1995 reissue.

Alone Together, Clifford Brown and Max Roach, Mercury Music, 1995.

M'Boom, Columbia/Legacy, 1979.

To the Max, a two-disc set (with two solos by Max Roach, among other tracks), Mesa/Blue Moon, 1991.

Chano Pozo

Diz and Bird at Carnegie Hall, September 29, 1947; features Chano Pozo on congas
playing "Cubano Be, Cubano Bop," Roost.

Max + Dizzy—Paris 1989, A&M Records, 1990.

Art Blakey

Blakey recorded with Billy Eckstine's band—primarily on tapings taken from the
radio in the 1940s, and with pianist Thelonious Monk as a sideman for Blakey on
the Atlantic label, and in many other groups. The bins are filled with recordings of
Art Blakey and the Jazz Messengers. Among the notable Messengers albums, not
only because of Blakey's work but for the sidemen whose careers he launched, are
the following:

Like Someone in Love, with trumpeter Lee Morgan, tenor saxophinst Wayne Shorter, pianist Bobby Timmons, bassist Jymie Merritt, Blue Note, 1960.

Three Blind Mice, Vol. 1, with trumpeter Freddie Hubbard, tenor saxophonist
Wayne Shorter, trombonist Curtis Fuller, pianist Cedar Walton, bassist Jymie
Merritt, Blue Note.

Free for All, with same personnel as above, except for bassist Reggie Workman,
Blue Note.

Mosaic, Blue Note, 1961.

A Night at Birdland, Vol. 1, CDP, 1987.

Orgy in Rhythm, Vols. 1 and 2, with Blakey, leader, and Art Taylor, Jo Jones, Specs
Wright, and others, Blue Note.

Roy Haynes

His recording *Bird at St. Nick's*, done in Charlie Parker's group on February 18,
1950, is sometimes available.

Te Vou!, with alto saxophonist Donald Harrison, guitarist Pat Metheny, pianist
Dave Kikoski, and bassist Christian McBride, Disques Dreyfus.

We Three, led by Haynes with pianist Phineas Newborn and bassist Paul Chambers
recorded on November 14, 1958, remastered Prestige/New Jazz, 1992.

John Coltrane's *Dear Old Stockholm*, Impulse!, 1965.

Chick Corea's *Now He Sings, Now He Sobs*, Blue Note, 1968.

Chick Corea and Friends' *Remembering Bud Powell*, Stretch, 1997.

Vernel Fournier

This New Orleans-born drummer became prominent in pianist Ahmad Jamal's trio, with bassist Israel Crosby, for such tunes as "Poinciana."

But Not for Me: Live at the Pershing, recorded at the Pershing Club, Chicago, on January 16, 1958, Chess Records.

Drummers with Miles Davis's groups in the 1950s and 1960s

This list is a taste of the many albums from Davis's exceptionally creative and fertile period as a mainstream jazz leader in the 1950s and 1960s.

Jimmy Cobb, *Kind of Blue*, includes "All Blues," Columbia, 1959.

Philly Joe Jones, *Milestones*, Columbia, 1958; *Cookin'*, Original Jazz Classics, 1956; *Porgy and Bess*, Columbia/Legacy, 1958.

Max Roach and Kenny Clarke, *Birth of the Cool*, Capitol/EMI, 1950.

Tony Williams, *Miles in the Sky*, Columbia/Legacy, 1968; *In a Silent Way*, Columbia, 1969; *The Sorcerer*, Columbia, 1967; *Miles Smiles*, Columbia, 1966; *E.S.P.*, Columbia Legacy, 1965.

Paul Motian

Waltz for Debbie, with Bill Evans as leader, OJC, 1961.

Sunday at the Village Vanguard (formerly called *The Village Vanguard Sessions*) with pianist Bill Evans as leader, and bassist Scott LaFaro, OJC, 1961.

Elvin Jones

Jones became famous in saxophonist John Coltrane's group in the 1960s and later led his own groups. Among the important Coltrane albums featuring Jones are: *Impressions*, Charly Records, 1992, cuts of which were included on *The Complete Village Vanguard Recordings of John Coltrane*, Impulse!, 1997; *Transition*, Impulse!, 1993;

Coltrane Plays the Blues, Atlantic Jazz; *My Favorite Things*, Atlantic, 1961; *A Love Supreme*, Impulse!, 1964, MCA, 1995, and GRP Records, 1995. For another side of the group's sound, as accompanist for a singer, listen to *John Coltrane-Johnny Hartman*, Impulse!, MCA Records, 1995; and *Ballads*, Impulse!, 1962.

Jack DeJohnette

DeJohnette, who drew attention to himself in a Miles Davis group that recorded *Bitches Brew* in 1969, later led his own group called *Special Edition*, which recorded the following:

Album Album, ECM, 1984.

Irresistible Forces, including alto saxophonist Greg Osby, GRP.

Works, ECM, 1994.

Keith Jarrett's Standards, Vol. 1, ECM, 1983, and Vol. 2, ECM, 1985.

Tony Williams

Eric Dolphy's *Out to Lunch*, Blue Note, 1964.

Lifetime: The Collection, Columbia/Legacy, Sony Music, 1992.

The Best of Tony Williams: The Blue Note Years, 1966.

Spectrum Anthology, Verve, 1997. This album was released right after Williams died.

Billy Higgins

Ornette Coleman's *The Shape of Jazz to Come*, Atlantic, 1959.

Ornette Coleman's *Free Jazz*, a double quartet album, with Higgins and drummer Ed Blackwell, Rhino Records, 1961.

Higgins is also well known for his work in mainstream jazz groups such as trio recordings led by pianist Cedar Walton.

FOR MORE INFORMATION

Books

Balliett, Whitney, *American Musicians: 56 Portraits in Jazz* (New York: Oxford University Press, New York, 1986).

Blades, James, and Johnny Dean, *How to Play Drums* (New York: St. Martin's Press, 1992).

Dodds, Baby, as told to Larry Gara, *The Baby Dodds Story*, revised edition (Baton Rouge: Louisiana State University Press, 1992).

Giddins, Gary, *Rhythm-a-ning-Jazz Tradition and Innovation in the '80s* (New York: Oxford University Press, 1985).

Gillespie, Dizzy, with Al Fraser, *To Be or Not to Bop* (New York: Doubleday, 1979).

Hasse, John Edward, *Beyond Category: The Life and Genius of Duke Ellington* (New York: Simon & Schuster, 1993).

Hennessey, Mike, *Klook* (New York: Quartet Books, 1990).

Haydon, Geoffrey, and Dennis Marks, editors, *Repercussions: A Celebration of African-American Music* (London: Century Publishing, 1985).

Kernfeld, Barry, editor, *The New Grove Dictionary of Jazz* (New York: St. Martin's Press, New York, 1995).

Korall, Burt, *Drummin' Men* (New York: Schirmer Books, 1990).

Lyons, Len, *The 101 Best Jazz Albums* (New York: William Morrow, 1980).

Simon, George T., *The Big Bands*, fourth edition (New York: Schirmer Books, 1981).

Spagnardi, Ron, *The Great Jazz Drummers* (Cedar Grove, NJ: Modern Drummer Publications, 1992).

KEEPERS 140

Stearns, Marshall W., *The Story of Jazz* (New York: Oxford University Press 1956; revised paperback edition, 1970).

Taylor, Arthur, *Notes and Tones* (New York: Perigee Books, 1977).

Tormé, Mel, *Traps: The Drum Wonder—the Life of Buddy Rich* (New York: Oxford University Press, 1991).

Periodicals

Jazz Times
8737 Colesville Road, 5th floor
Silver Spring, Maryland 20910-3921
Phone 301-588-4114
Fax 301-588-2009

Down Beat
102 North Haven Road
Elmhurst, Illinois 60126-2970
Phone 630-941-2030
Fax 630-941-3210

Jazz Iz
3620 N.W. 43rd Street
Gainesville, Florida 32606-8103
Phone 352-375-3705
Fax 352-375-7268

In New York City, a little monthly magazine called *Hot House* is distributed free of charge in jazz clubs and contains listings of all the players in the region's clubs for the month, plus at least two profiles of musicians appearing in town that month. For back issues, which may be available for a small charge, write:

Gene Kalbacher, editor and publisher
18 Whippoorwill Lane
Rockaway Township, New Jersey 07866
Phone 201-627-5349

Internet Sites

Jazz 52nd Street

http://www.52ndstreet.com/

The Internet's largest CD jazz review site contains more than eight hundred reviews.

Jazz Central Station

http://www.jazzcentralstation.com

Includes dates of upcoming jazz concerts and festivals, as well as a wide range of jazz-related information.

Jazz Corner

http://www.jazzcorner.com/index.html

Features information about musicians and organizations, concerts and club dates, the business of jazz, and a chat room.

Jazz Institute of Chicago

http://www.JazzInstituteOfChicago.org/

Numerous articles on jazz personalities and histories, as well as a performance calendar.

Jazz Online

http://www.jazzonln.com/

A central site for reviews, interviews, and news; includes a vast database of audio and video clips of contemporary jazz musicians.

INDEX

Numbers in *italics* indicate illustrations.

Abstract jazz, 113
Accompanying technique, 50
Acoustic jazz, 124
Africa, drumming in, 9
African-Americans, 52, 71
Afro-Cuban music, 88-89
"After You've Gone," 21
Alcoholism, 23, 29, 35, 40, 75
Ali, Rashied, 123
"All Blues," 114
Alternative Festival, 75
Anderson, Ivie, 44
Apollo Theatre, 73, 95, 100
Armstrong, Louis, 7, 21, 23, 28-29, 30, 46

The Baby Dodds Story, 21
Baker, Chet, 104
Balliett, Whitney, 41, 50, 56, 58, 118, 120, 121
Barbarin, Paul, 34
Basie, Count, 12-13, *12*, 59
Bass drum, 12-13, 54
Bauduc, Ray, 35-36, *35*, *37*
Bauza, Mario, 89
Beason, Bill, 62
Bebop, 9, 13, 63-77, 82
   debut of, 69
   melodies of, 65-66
Bechet, Sidney, 20
Bellson, Louis, 38
Benford, Tommy, 62
Berimbau, 123
Best, Denzil, 62
Biff shot, 27
Billy the Kid, 76
Birdland (club), 100
Birth of the Cool, 82, 104
Bitches Brew, 121
Blackman, Cindy, 87, 126
Blackwell, Ed, 122
Blakey, Art, 9, 65, 72, 84, 87, 94-98, *95*
   and the Jazz Messengers, 94, 96-97
Blanton, Jimmy, 65
Bock, Richard, 104
Boland, Francy, 69
"Bombs" in drumming, 13, 65
Boogie-woogie style, 39
"Boplicity," 82, 104
Brackeen, Joanne, 97

Bradley, Will, 39
Brooks, Roy, 84
Brown, Clifford, 75
Brushes, 14, 49
Buddy's Place (club), 58

Cafe Society, 36, 102, 110
Calfskin drumheads, 14, 19-20
California sound, 104-105
Carmen Jones, 75
Carnegie Hall, 52
Carrington, Terri Lyne, 87, 125, *126*
Carson, Johnny, 59
Carter, Benny, 74
Catlett, Big Sid, 46, 49-52, *51*, 73, 80, 81, 110
"The Celery Stalks at Midnight," 39
Chord structure, 67, 82, 114
Christian, Charlie, 65
Civil rights movement, 112-113
Clarke-Boland Big Band, 69
Clarke, Kenny, 63, 64, 65, *66*, 67-69, 71, 81
Clave (rhythm), 91
Cobb, Jimmy, 114, 115
Cole, Cozy, *45*, 45-47, 80
Coleman, Ornette, 86, 113, 114
Coltrane, John, 113-114, 118
Conga/Conguero drum, 91
Cool jazz, 13, 104-108
Cotton Club, 44
Cowbells, 18-19
Crawford, Jimmy, 36-37
Crosby, Bob, 36
Crosby, Israel, 83
Cuban music, 88-91
   instruments of, 90
Cuerica, Sylvia, 126
Cymbals, 12-15, 28, 34
   nuances of, 54
Cyrille, Andrew, 123

Davis, Miles, 74, 82, 87, 104, 113-14, 115
DeJohnette, Jack, 85, 121
Dickerson, Carrol, 21
Dodds, Warren Baby, 13, 14, 18-21, *19*, 23, 25-31, *26*, 79
Dolphy, Eric, 107
Dorsey, Jimmy, 38
Dorsey, Tommy, 38, 41, 56-57, *79*
Down Beat (magazine), 36, 108
   Talent Deserving Wider Recognition category, 98

Drug addiction, 75
Drumming, 9-10, 27
   techniques, 11-13
   terms used in, 27
Drum sets, 9, 4, 16, 44-45, 48, 60, 72
   decoration of, 16
   heads, 14, 19-20, 42, 105-106
   pieces, 9, 14-15, 16-17, 60
   rims of, 14, 18
Drumsticks, 14

Eckstine, Billy, 58, 96
Eldridge, Roy, 21, 53-54
Electric instruments, 16
Electronic equipment, 116
Ellington, Duke, 15-16, *15*, 42-45, 64, 74, 82
"Epistrophy," 69
Esquire (magazine), 39
Eubanks, Kevin, *95*
Evans, Gil, 82, 104

Fatool, Nick, 38
"Feather" stroke, 11, 12, 13
Fields, Kansas, 62
"52nd Street Theme," 69
Fitzgerald, Ella, 47
Five Spot Cafe, 86, 100
Flam/flim-flam, 27, 78
Flatted fifth tone, 65, 67
Foster, Pops, 27-28
4/4 time, 10, 37, 56, 82
Fournier, Vernel, 83-84
Fox, Charles, 73
Francis, Panama, 62
Free jazz, 11, 13, 86, 87, 122
Freeman, Bud, 29
Fuller, Walter Gil, 89
Fusion music, 76, 86, 121

Gadd, Steve, 87
Giants of Jazz, 98
Gillespie, Dizzy, 63-64, 68, 69, 77, 96
   and Latin music, 88-92
The Glenn Miller Story, 7, 34, 46
Goodman, Benny, 7-8, *8*, 29, 40-41, 47, 51-52
Goodman, Saul, 46
Gordon, Max, 75
Grace note (flam), 78
Granz, Norman, 57

Greatest Jazz Concert Ever, 71
Greer, Sonny, 15-16, *15*, 42-45, *43*, 80
Gretsch drums, 48

Haggart, Bob, 36
Hamilton, Chico, 83, 104-108, *106*
Hancock, Herbie, 116
Hard bop, 13, 84, 93-103
Harvey, Jane, *57*
Hayes, Louis, 85
Haynes, Roy, 85, 93, 95, 98-103, *101*
Heard, J.C., 39-40
Heath, Percy, *109*, 109-111
Heath, Tootie, 111
Henderson, Fletcher, 37, 80
Herman, Woody, 41-42
Higgins, Billy, 86, 122, *122*
Hi-hat cymbal, 19, 23, 37, 79
Hill, Teddy, 68
Hines, Earl, 21, 50
Hip Ensemble, 102
Holiday, Billie, *51*

Improvisation, 11, 34, 76

Jackson, Chubby, 42
Jackson, Milt, 69, 109-111, *109*
Jamal, Ahmad, 83
Jazz at the Philharmonic, 55, 57, 74
Jazz drumming, 10-11
    functions of, 11
    overview of, 78-87
Jazz Times (magazine), 116
Johnson, Bunk, 10
Johnson, Gus, 62
Johnson, Lyndon B., 113
Johnson, Otis, 62
Johnson, Walter, 37, 80
Jones, Elvin, 13, 84, *84*, 118-119, *119*
Jones, Hank, 119
Jones, Papa Jo, 12-13, *12*, 59-62, *61*, 65, 73, 80, 81, *101*
Jones, Philly Joe, 85, 93, 114
Jones, Thad, 83, 119

Kahn, Tiny, 62
Kay, Connie, 85, 109-111, *109*
Kennedy, John F., 112-113
Kennedy, Robert F., 113
King Creole's Jazz Band, *19*
King, Martin Luther, Jr., 113
King Rex parade, 10
King, Stan, 35
Kirby, John, 73

"Klook" (Clarke), 68
Krupa, Gene, 7-8, *8*, 24, 31, 46, 47, 49, 52-56, *53*, 79, *79*
    heart trouble of, 58

Latin drummers, 88-92
Laveau, Marie, 9
Leedy Company drums, 45
Leeman, Cliff, 62
Levey, Stan, 82, 93
Lewis, John, 69, 85, 108-111, *109*
Lewis, Mel, 18, 20, 24, 34-35, 49, 83
Lewis, Victor, 125
Lick (technique), 27
Loudness, 113, 117-118
Ludwig, William, 28
Lunceford, Jimmy, 36
Lyons, Len, 9, 81

Mackrell, Dennis, 87, 125
Make Mine Music, 46
Mallet instruments, 76
Manne, Shelley, 83
Mantilla, Ray, 91
Marable, Fate, 21, 28
March rhythms, 10
Mardi Gras Carnival, 10
Maricle, Sherrie, 126
Marijuana, 54-55
Marsala, Joe, 56
Marsalis, Branford, *95*
Marsalis, Wynton, 124, 125
Marshall, Kaiser, 34, 80
Martin, Henry, 27
Max Plus Dizzy, 77
M'Boom Re: Percussion, 76, 92
McKinley, Ray, 37-39
McRae, Carmen, 68
Measures (bars), 10
Melodic drumming, 8
Metronome (magazine), 41
Metropole (club), 55
Miller, Glenn, 7, 34, 37
Mingus, Charles, 71
Minton's Playhouse, 68, 74, 81
Mitchell, Red, 104
Modal music/modes, 114
Modern Jazz Quartet (MJQ), 69, 85, 108-111, *109*
Monk, Thelonious, 16, 64, 67, 81, 93
Moore, Ralph, 103
Morera, Airto, 123
Motian, Paul, 86, *86*
Moye, Famoudou Don, 123

Mulligan, Gerry, 83, 104-105
Muslim religion, 68, 72

Nash, Louis, 87, 125
New Orleans, 9, 10-11
Newport Jazz Festival, 75, 98, 107
"New thing," 86
Notes and Tones, 94

O'Day, Anita, 53, *53*
Offbeats (technique), 42
Okeh label, 21
Oliver, Joe "King," 29-31
Onyx Club, 69, 74
Ory, Kid, 27

Palmer, Robert, 81
Paradiddle, 78
Paramount Theater, 55
Parker, Charlie, 63-64, 81
Pedal tom-tom, 36
Percussionists, 11
Pettiford, Oscar, 69
Pickup (downbeat), 27
Pitch, 9
"Playing in two," 11
Political activism, 71, 75, 112-113
Pollack, Ben, 29, 31, 33-34
Polyrhythmic style, 10, 65, 73, 88
Pozo, Chavo, 88-90
Press roll, 20, 21, 98
Progressive jazz, 63
Puente, Tito, 92, *92*

Quebec, Ike, 98

Racial segregation, 28, 36, 38, 44, 68, 74, *77*, 95
Ragtime, 10
Ratamacue, 78
Redcross, Bob, 96
Rent parties, 72
Rich, Buddy, 56-59, *57*, 80
Richmond, Danny, 123
Ride cymbal, 98
Riley, Ben, 16
Roach, Max, 9, 65, 69, *70*, 71-77, 81, *83*
    political activism of, 75
Roach, Maxine, 76
Rock and roll, 113, 124
Roll (technique), 78, 121
Rudiments, 27, 78
Russell, George, 89
Russell, Luis, 34, 100

Salsa, 91
Sampson, Edgar, 49
Savoy Ballroom, 47, 100
Sbarbaro, Tony, 62
Scat language, 96
Schoenberg, Loren, 18, 34, 49
Second line funerals, 10-11, 24
The Shape of Jazz to Come, 122
Shaw, Artie, 41
Sheila E, 125
Signatures (times), 10
Silver, Horace, 96
Simon, George T., 54, 56
Sinatra, Frank, 57
"Sing Sing Sing," 49, 52
Singleton, Arthur Zutty, 21, 22, 23-24, 31, 79
The Skin You Love to Touch, 107
Smith, Marvin "Smitty," 16, 87, 124
Son montuno music, 91
Spencer, O'Neil, 62, 73
Spyro Gyra, 123
Stacy, Jess, 29
Stafford, George, 34
Storyville (club), 27

Streckfus, 28
Sweatman, Wilbur, 46
Swing-era drumming, 15-16, 40-62
    explanation of, 55
Swing ragtime, 10
Swing Street, 40
Syncopation, 10-11

"Talking" on drums, 9
Tate, Grady, 60, 62
Taylor, Art, 94
Teagarden, Jack, 37
Teschemacher, Fran, 29
Thigpen, Ed, 82
Third Stream music, 13, 82, 85, 108-111
Thornhill, Claude, 82, 104
Three Deuces, 74
Timekeeping, 11, 13, 120
To Be or Not to Bop, 64, 89
Toddle time, 28-29
Tones, 9
Tough, Davey, 29, 40-42, 80, 80
Traps, 28

Uptown House, 64, 74

Uptown String Quartet, 76
Vasconcelos, Nano, 123
Vaughan, Sarah, 99, 114
Vietnam War, 113
Village Vanguard (club), 75, 83
Voodoo, 9

Walcott, Colin, 123
Washington, Kenny, 50, 52, 87, 125
Weather Report, 123
Webb, Chick, 37, 47-49, *48*, 73, 80
Wein, George, 75, 98
West, Alvy, 57
Wettling, George, 29, 32-33, 33
Whiteman, Paul, 29
Williams, Tony, 85, 85, 115-118
Wilson, Shadow, 93
WKCR radio, 18, 20, 34, 49
Women drummers, 87, 97, 125-126
Wong, Herb, 116
Woodyard, Sam, 62

Yellowjackets, 123
Yoruba religion, 91
Young, Lester, 60, 62, 64, 73

ABOUT THE AUTHOR

Leslie Gourse has researched and written stories for various mediums, including CBS, *The New York Times*, *The Los Angeles Times*, and *The Boston Globe*. Her articles have appeared in magazines and newspapers, covering general culture, social trends, and music. Her books, including *Dizzy Gillespie and the Birth of Bebop* and *The Triumph and Tragedy of Lady Day*, have earned high praise from the critics. For Franklin Watts, Ms. Gourse is the author of the entire Art of Jazz series, including these titles: *Blowing on the Changes: The Art of the Jazz Horn Players; Deep Down in Music: The Art of the Great Jazz Bassists; Striders to Beboppers and Beyond: The Art of the Jazz Piano; Swingers and Crooners: The Art of Jazz Singing;* and *Timekeepers: The Great Jazz Drummers.*